RIDING THE ELEPHANT

SURVIVING AND LOVING IN A BIPOLAR MARRIAGE

CATHARINE MCKENTY

INTRODUCTION BY ALAN HUSTAK

Torchflame Books

Durham, NC

Copyright © 2019 Catharine McKenty
Riding the Elephant: surviving and loving in a bipolar marriage
Catharine McKenty
www.neilmckenty.com

Published 2019, by Torchflame Books
www.torchflamebooks.com
Durham, NC 27713 USA
SAN: 920-9298

Paperback ISBN: 978-1-61153-346-0
E-book ISBN: 978-1-61153-347-7
Library of Congress Control Number: 2019945720

ALL RIGHTS RESERVED
No part of this publication may be reproduced, stored in a retrieval system, or transmitted in any form or by any means, electronic, mechanical, photocopying, recording, scanning, or otherwise, except as permitted under Section 107 or 108 of the 1976 International Copyright Act, without the prior written permission except in brief quotations embodied in critical articles and reviews.

When you take on an impossible task,
the universe conspires to help you.
—Johann Wolfgang von Goethe

CONTENTS

INTRODUCTION

As Catharine McKenty approaches her 90th birthday she has at last fully found a voice of her own.

Her late husband, Neil McKenty, was one of Montreal's highest-rated radio talk show hosts. His open line talk show, *Exchange*, which ran on CJAD during the '70s, became a sort of public confessional where listeners exchanged ideas in an atmosphere of civility. With him she co-authored a best-selling book about the history of the Laurentian Lodge Ski Club. She acted as his right-hand during the intense months of writing the John Main biography, *In the Stillness Dancing*. On her own she mined her family's rich Irish history for her engaging tale, *Polly of Bridgewater Farm*. But during their 40 years of marriage Neil was the outspoken voice of the family.

Catharine was every inch Neil's intellectual equal. She had an Honour's degree in English from Victoria College at the University of Toronto, studying under Northrop Frye. After the war she spent four years in reconciliation work with people from all over Europe, with winters in Germany during its reconstruction. She worked as a research editor for *Pace* magazine in Los Angeles and as a speechwriter for Ontario's Minister of Education.

Catharine has never ridden an elephant, but she lived with an elephant in the room, the illness no one talked about.

Two years after she married Neil, Catharine was shocked to discover that her husband had had a history of mental illness. She also understood that Neil was a man who was used to getting his own way, who "had very little idea of the give and take of relationships."

Their marriage should not have worked, but it did. Both deeply spiritual people in their own way, she accepted the challenge of coping with his deep-seated depression and unpredictable bipolar behaviour.

Any number of books have been written about depression. Neil even wrote about it in his autobiography, *The Inside Story*. Catharine views it from the outside. With this book Catharine returns to her distinguished family's Irish roots and writes about what only she could know about her husband's illness and how her ancestry helped her cope. As she writes, "she grew up with people who were not quitters." She was not only Neil's wife but his guardian angel, confident that she would find the strength when she needed it to make the marriage work.

Catharine is deceptively tough. She is a true original with a shrewd understanding of people. She can be demanding. Since Neil's death in 2012 she has been relentless in her efforts to keep his memory alive and at the same time help provide a nuanced understanding of his condition so others can better understand the bipolar condition.

"We need more stories of hope in this world," she has written. "Neil's story and mine, intertwined for forty years are each, in their own way, stories of hope in spite of unsettling challenges."

—Alan Hustak

EARLY YEARS – TORONTO 1930 - 1952

I was fortunate to grow up on a farm at the western edge of Toronto, on Don Mills Road.

The household included a grandmother who was involved in medical services for women in India, my mother who had spent two years in China learning Mandarin, several aunts, an uncle, and fifty-six cows kept in line by a couple of bossy bulls. There were also cats, squirrels, and tiny chipmunks. One of my earliest memories is of a little nest of baby rabbits snuggling together at the base of a corn stook, with killdeer calling over the cornfield.

The Don River ran right through the farm, with a maple wood on its bank. That land is now covered in concrete—except for seventeen acres recently bought by the Aga Khan.

As I think about my childhood, an image arises in my mind. It was my grandmother's living room, the afternoon sunlight streaming in through the west window. A fire was crackling in the stone fireplace. A plate of cinnamon toast and a covered silver dish full of hot, buttered crumpets were set out near the green Aynsley china tea set. This room was the stage setting for the comings and goings of an extended family whose lives would interweave with mine in an ongoing story.

The living room was the heart of a deep-cellared, oblong house built of rose-grey fieldstone, set in nine hundred acres of rolling Ontario farmland. In 1930, when my young widowed mother brought me there as a baby, the farm was eight miles outside the Toronto city limits. The house was set on a slight rise on the west side of Don Mills Road, giving it a commanding view of the surrounding countryside. The Eglinton Avenue bridge had not yet been built. During the Depression, a steady stream of homeless men found work in the fields.

I don't think the places and people we have loved ever cease to be part of us. Quantum physicists tell us those connections continue on as part of a mysterious whole that surrounds us and expresses itself through us.

To this day whenever I see a sign for North on a highway, a huge cow barn with 56 black-and-white Holstein cows is right there, superimposed on whatever other North images I've acquired since. East is irrevocably the great maple woods at the back of the farm, with the early morning sun rising over a Don River valley that was filled with violets and trilliums every spring.

South is cornfields stretching to the horizon, marked off by old wooden fences. West is Grandmother's living room with the setting sun stirring up a bunch of lazy flies droning on the window sill, and refracting dancing points of colour from the French prisms on the mantelpiece.

My own deepest connection with the earth goes back to those first ten years of my life. From the time I was four, I spent hours riding on a wheel rim of the old red Massey Harris tractor driven by toothless Angus McNab. Angus had worked as a shepherd in Scotland, came out to Canada, met my grandfather, and became foreman of Grandfather's farm. I spent happy hours in total silence while Angus ploughed one perfect furrow after another of the farm's upper fields. I can still hear the sound of the plough's gearshift releasing at the end of a furrow, the chug of the engine as it lumbered around to plough in the opposite direction. Angus had a serene radiance in his face and he smiled his toothless smile as he worked wordlessly until the sun went down.

I would stop off at the barns to see the cows being milked, or pet the cats that came streaking along when a pail of foaming milk was kicked over. Often I spent time patting the soft noses of the calves as I offered them a carrot. Then I went tight-rope walking over the long ploughed furrows, listening to the wind singing in the telephone wires.

In spring the farmhands tapped the maple trees that sloped down to the Don River. Maple syrup was always available whenever we had porridge or pancakes. Needless to say, years later, at Beauty's restaurant in Montreal, there was no question whether I would have maple syrup on my pancakes while my parsimonious husband insisted on using the house table syrup, thus saving a dollar.

One early spring day during my childhood I went skipping alone down to the lower garden. There in the shelter of a single volcanic rock was a patch of earth warmed by the sun, with the melting snow banked around it. A single blue flower, a scilla, blossomed in the brown earth. I had the strongest feeling this jaunty little flower was trying to tell me something that I couldn't quite understand.

Years later, it occurred to me that it was saying, "Bloom for the day."

Eighty years later I am still listening.

At the heart of Donlands was my Irish grandmother, Lydia Orford Fleming. People who met her for the first time were sometimes intimidated. With her erect posture, beautiful skin and full crown of silvery-white hair, she was sometimes known as "the duchess." Many more knew her simply as their friend and often as their friend in times of need. Her eight children had found her strict. I experienced the gentler side of her.

At Donlands farm in the spring, my beloved Granny Fleming would hold my five-year-old hand as she inspected her flowerbeds. I remember the first tulip bud poking its head up through the earth. Later, turnips, potatoes and carrots would land up in the root cellar under the house. It was unknown then for families like ours to buy vegetables from California. You ate what you grew and could store.

Donlands Farm

When my widowed Mum and I came to live in that mainly adult household, word went out, "This child will not be spoiled." But when my grandmother put me in a corner for some misdemeanor, I thought to myself, "She didn't really mean it." When I came out of the corner I would go down to the lower field to see the first asparagus shoots appearing in the soil, or lean out the window of my tiny bedroom to breathe in the smell of lilac.

I was allowed to spend a surprising amount of time accompanied only by my Airedale dog, Fieldy, alone out-of-doors, wandering over the fields, or lying on my back on the warm earth in the shadow of a large field stone, trying to get a cloud above my head to move along with an imaginary push of my hand.

On other days I visited Uncle Murray's magnificent horses in the long grey barn at the back of the farm. He and his sister Agnes had both won prizes for jumping in their younger days.

Living room at Donlands Farm, 1931. Catharine's mother Victoria, Aunt Reba (standing), Granny Fleming and baby Catharine, with Grandfather R.J.'s portrait over the fireplace, flanked by the prisms that refracted the afternoon light.

To my enchantment, another child just my size suddenly appeared to share in my delights. Her name was Lydia, like my grandmother, only child of Aunt Agnes and Uncle Eric. She had an irrepressible sense of fun. She and her mother would sometimes get the giggles, to my great astonishment. No one else at Donlands did such a thing. All the family remembered when Aunt Agnes, as a child, got a fit of giggles at the big mahogany table at St. Clair Avenue. "Get down immediately, baby!" roared Grandfather, instructing her to leave the table. Now the giggles were back, in a household where children were still expected to be seen and not heard.

Together Lydia and I were a match for any grown-up, no matter how strict. We raced around madly on our tricycles on the big verandah at the back of the house and invented a game called 'Hiding from grown-ups.' Giggling hysterically we would peek through banisters, hide in linen closets and appear for a supper of brown bread and fresh cow's milk at the last possible moment. One time Uncle Murray put us up on the back of his pony. We laughed so hard that we slid off, no damage done except dust on our clothes.

After Lydia left, I was once again the only child. The grownups had dinner in the evening at the great mahogany dining table in the long dining room with the glass doors looking out at Grandmother's garden. I was not allowed to eat with them but was given an early supper alone in a room with only my teddy bear for company. Supper was often a dish of hot milk with squares of brown and white bread broken into it. When the dishes were being cleared after the first course, my mother would excuse herself and slip upstairs to tuck me in. She would say she was "putting in the sleeping-winkers" as she pressed my eyelids. Then she would whisper the words of King David in his Psalm 23.

> The Lord is my shepherd; I shall not want.
>
> He maketh me to lie down in green pastures; he leadeth me beside still waters.
>
> He restoreth my soul: he leadeth me in the paths of righteousness for his name's sake.
>
> Yea, though I walk through the valley of the shadow of death, I will fear no evil: for thou art with me; thy rod and thy staff comfort me.
>
> Thou preparest a table before me in the presence of mine enemies: thou annointest my head with oil; my cup runneth over.
>
> Surely goodness and mercy shall follow me all the days of my life: and I will dwell in the house of the Lord forever.

Of course I had wonderful moments with my mother all during those years. Her room was just down the hall from mine and I was always welcome. But she was also under the thumb of her older sister Reba, and a little uncertain of her role as a mother.

Very early in life, I realized that other children had a father and I didn't. This included most of my cousins. In 1935, just before my sixth birthday, I entered kindergarten at Bishop Strachan School, a noble and very strict school for girls. There, almost all my classmates seemed to have fathers who were very present in their lives.

My older cousin Bob had a vivid memory of the summer of 1929, following my parents' July wedding, when Dad took him and his brother fishing out in a deeper part of the lake. Off they went in Dad's sturdy Peterborough canoe. Bob remembered the strong sense of connection he felt that was missing with his own father.

The grown-ups at Donlands must have had a hard time knowing what to say to me about my father. For my mother the grief was still too present. Then one evening the silent movie of my parents' wedding was to be shown in the living room at Donlands. For the first time I would be able to see my father as others had seen him.

At the last minute, a decision was made by my elders that I was to be sent to bed instead. Imagine my fury and heartbreak. I suppose they were afraid I'd be upset or haunted by the image; so little was known then about grief therapy. Something closed down in me. The whole idea of my father became like a frozen river in my innermost being, not to be talked about until I became an adult. It was only much later that I realized how lucky I was to be raised by a courageous mother who made a life for both of us at a time when it was not easy for single women. It was a full eighty years later that I finally saw that film.

My father, Walter Turnbull, was a man with a radiant faith in God that communicated itself to all who knew him. As a boy, he was a real rebel. His father had walked out of the local Baptist Church with his four tall sons when the sermon had proved too narrow-minded for his progressive approach. He founded another Baptist church in their hometown of Peterborough, Ontario where all Christians were welcome. Dad was given a basket of apples to take to the new minister from the single apple tree in the backyard of the house where he grew up. The minister reported with a wink that a bite had been taken out of each apple. That apple tree also allowed Dad and his brothers to climb out of the bedroom window at night.

Dad would paddle out in the Peterborough canoe at the cottage, then throw himself overboard with a great war whoop to scare his mother. Later he tried that trick from a boat on the Hudson River near Nyack, NY, and nearly drowned in the swift current.

After high school, Dad studied theology at McMaster College in Hamilton, Ontario. The student yearbook quotes his wish to "sail beyond the sunset," which indeed he did. He visited missions in China and other Asian countries. He walked on foot through Peru looking for places to found a mission. Off the coast there was a Russian ship with a complete radio station on it. Somehow he corralled that radio station and had it brought back to New York to broadcast a message of hope, love and forgiveness back to South America. Later he would write to my mother that her eyes reminded him of the blue of Lake Titicaca in Peru.

Grandmother in India with two daughters and a daughter-in-law

I got my love of travelling from both sides of the family. In the early years of the twentieth century, my maternal Grandmother liked to ride elephants. An ivory string of them marched across the radiator in her living room, trunk curled around tail. And if you let her out of your sight, she was likely to end up on a camel in an Egyptian desert taking in the Sphinx. A postcard she sent to her nieces from India carries a photo of her, majestically perched on the back of a huge elephant. Beside her sits her rebellious daughter Evelyn and a daughter-in-law who stares sombrely at the camera. This was not their idea. On the back of the card she wrote to her nieces,

"Dear Annie and Lizzie,

What do you think of our mode of conveyance? It gave me a great thrill to go up a steep hill mounted thus — camels, peacocks, monkeys here are very numerous — an everyday sight. This is being a wonderful experience for us all. There will be much to tell on return home."

Granny always had much to tell. In the early morning, when only the two of us were awake, I would go down the hall to her room and snuggle down beside her under the big eiderdown that smelled of lavender. She would share a sip from her thermos of hot water with me and we would chatter away. Stories about the magic of India and China would begin there in the bedroom, and end later around the fire downstairs. I remember a charming photo of her in China roaring along in a rickshaw. Once on her way home from India, she stopped off in Egypt to see the pyramids. From there she brought home an unusual watercolour of a Bedouin kneeling in the desert in silent prayer, with his camel standing nearby in complete stillness. The picture hung on the wall above the green horsehair sofa, opposite the fireplace in the living room at Donlands. I often sat on that sofa, communing with the picture. Today it hangs in a place of honour in my own room, where it catches the light.

In 1935 she found herself going up the Yangtze River in China to visit her daughter who had married a Presbyterian missionary. The scenery was spectacular and the only available mode of transport was a narrow, rickety boat. Passengers were obliged to carry all their money with them in the form of heavy coins in order to buy food for their journey. There was a famine in the area. All their coins were hidden in the thatched roof of the boat. Suddenly a gang of fierce-looking bandits brandishing swords appeared from nowhere, demanding that they stop. Grandmother and my mother, who had come with her on this trip, prayed heartily. The bandits took all the food on the boat and vanished.

Later I learned more about my grandmother and the serious side of her interest in India and China. As a young girl, she and a close friend, Rosalind Bell-Smith, daughter of the well-known watercolour artist Frederic Marlett Bell-Smith, worked (and played piano) in a Toronto inner city mission known as the Sackville Street Mission. Rosalind went to China as a missionary in her own right and as the wife of one of the pioneering Presbyterian missionaries of the time, Dr. Jonathan Goforth. Her letters to Grandmother Lydia from 1890 through 1913 paint a moving picture of the hardships and danger endured by those families.

At 17, Lydia married a promising young politician, Robert Fleming, an alderman who later became Mayor of Toronto. His first wife, Mary Jane Breadon of Montreal, had died leaving two children. The oldest, Rebecca, was not much younger than Lydia herself. When her father told her of his impending marriage, Reba exclaimed, "That angel!" about her new step-mother, my grandmother.

Robert, or R.J. as people called him, had been assisting Lydia's widowed mother. He advised her on property and kept in touch with her only son who repeatedly sold whatever he had, including his clothes, to buy alcohol. Eventually, Lydia's brother died of alcoholism in the Don Jail in Toronto. Lydia never spoke of him again. He was buried apart from the rest of the family. Even her own children believed she had been an only child.

Lydia and Robert were married in 1888 and lived at first on Parliament Street in Toronto. In 1886 Robert had supported Mayor William Holmes Howland in a municipal election whose central issue was the closing of half of the bars in Toronto. Doctors supported the cause, and living rooms all over town became hotbeds of political activity. Motivated by his own family's experience and the experiences of countless Irish families, R.J. threw himself into the temperance fray. They were up against powerful liquor interests. Families opposed to temperance, such as the Gooderhams, enlisted their fellow Anglicans. R.J. called on the Toronto Orangemen.

Cartoons of the day made hay with the comic side of the election. A marvellous, small volume called *The Methodist Bicycle Revolution* captures some of the flavour of the contest.

Other issues were of long-term concern to R.J. He had grown up in a Cabbagetown where many of the Irish families eked out a precarious existence. The area had been given that name after the many sturdy cabbages grown in the front yards. His sister had, like many other women, died in childbirth, intensifying the family hardships. He was passionate about the needs of working people. Beginning in his teens, he had built up a haying business. Then he bought houses to rent out and opened a real estate office. His letters show a man determined to lift his family out of the surrounding poverty. To a friend who had invited him to a concert he wrote, "I am unable to accept your kind invitation now or in the foreseeable future. At present, I am doing the work of two men."

In school he had gotten into a number of fights. Anyone who tried to cheat him soon recognized the error of their ways. In another letter, he admitted to a friend his gratitude that the Methodist Church and his sister Polly had taken hold of him. "Otherwise, I would have been in serious trouble." His Methodism reinforced his sense of justice. In 1892, during the first of his mayoralty campaigns, he became known as "the people's Bob." He successfully fought to raise the minimum wage for working people from ten to fifteen cents an hour.

He campaigned against the Toronto Street Railway, a monopoly, to get cheaper access to the waterfront for working families. Later, he fought Sir Adam Beck to keep hydro lines away from the waterfront which he insisted should be kept for public use. He lost on this issue, and he lost his ongoing struggle to get City Council to think ahead for the good of the whole city, with projects such as the widening of Yonge Street.

My mother was born in 1897, the year of Queen Victoria's Jubilee. She was named Alexandrina Victoria Fleming, and nicknamed "Queenie." City Council presented her father with a two-handled silver loving cup with her name on it. That year, he resigned as mayor to become Assessment Commissioner and earn some more money for his growing family.

During his years as mayor, the real estate boom came to an end. He had invested heavily in property and could not pay the taxes. His affairs were broadcast in all the newspapers. The contents of his household waste bin were scavenged to uncover material against him. Friends, including some of his political opponents, lent him money without interest. Years later, he paid back every cent with interest to his creditors or their widows. He never held a grudge. After a hard-fought election, he would shake hands with his opponent. But he said quietly to my mother, "Queenie, public life is a bruising and sometimes thankless affair." She remembered that Canada's Prime Minister Mackenzie King offered him any post he would take in his cabinet. He refused. No written proof exists of this offer, but my mother remembered hearing it more than once. She also remembered and internalized his often repeated injunction, "Queenie, think in large terms."

In 1899, R.J. and Lydia, with the help of Lydia's mother, Mrs. Orford, bought a property "way out in the country" for very little money. The house was at the corner of St. Clair and Bathurst, where there were no sidewalks and which was a field of mud in the spring. It had orchards and a ravine on one side. The reason for the move was that several of his children had become sick in the city. Also, the neighbours had objected to the smell of cows on Parliament Street, which R.J. insisted on keeping to provide fresh milk for his family. My mother, Victoria, talked about getting her white dress filthy from the mud of St. Clair Avenue. As the family grew, more wings and an ample verandah were added. A cherry orchard and vegetable beds surrounded two sides of the house.

L to R: GOLDIE, STELLA, RUSSELL, LLOYD, VICTORIA, MURRAY, EVELYN, AGNES, Toronto, 1905

Catharine's Fleming aunts and uncles as children
at their home on St Clair Avenue in Toronto, 1905

Later, the house was bought for an orphanage by Mother Irene, Head of the Sisters of Loretto, whom R.J. had advised on real estate matters. It was an interesting friendship for a Northern Irish Protestant whose children remained persistently suspicious of Rome even up to the time of my own marriage. The orphanage has since been replaced by a car wash, gas station and parking lot.

At Donlands farm, my mother and aunts often reminisced about growing up on St. Clair Avenue. There were never less than 30 people at Sunday tea, from the latest baby to my stately grandparents. Grandmother Lydia poured tea with great style while Grandfather R.J. answered questions about livestock and politics. R.J.'s older sister Polly and her husband John Verner came over from their house just across the street. Reba and younger brother Everett were old enough to pass around the tea cups, while my mother waited for the day that she would be old enough to handle the china cups. Uncle Murray was a rambunctious four-year-old, overseen by his older sister Stella. Mum's cousins Caul and Vern McAree were being raised by Aunt Polly after their mother died. Young Russell was the son who grew to share his father's passion for the care of livestock. There were plates full of cookies and sandwiches to accompany English tea.

Later, school friends arrived for skating parties on the ice rink or musical evenings with Uncle Russell playing the piano by ear. Paul Goforth, son of Aunt Stella's missionary friend Rosalind Goforth, arrived from China to spend his school years as part of the family. When the entire Salvation Army band went down with their ship in a storm, Grandfather R.J. offered to adopt one of the orphans. The whole house was turned into a hospital during a diphtheria epidemic.

Grandfather Fleming bought one of the first cars in Toronto, although he never learned to drive. His 12-year-old daughter Evelyn, however, was a superb driver, and would drive along King Street to pick up her father at his office. She had to sit on a cushion to see over the steering wheel. One day, a policeman asked her, "What on earth do you think you are doing?" She airily explained her purpose and he waved her on.

Usually, however, the children used a pony cart pulled by Rodney, a shaggy Shetland, who had appeared beside the Christmas tree one year with a red bow around his neck. They would fetch the mail dropped off by the train at Dupont Street, then head down University Avenue for a look at the lake.

Later, Uncle Murray would canter up to the house with the whole of the Hunt Club on horseback to salute his mother. A magnificent portrait of him dressed in his red hunting jacket, called "pinks" by those in the know, now hangs in Toronto's Hunt Club.

One day a company of two hundred soldiers arrived at St. Clair Avenue to salute my grandfather and ask for a drink of water. My mother said, "Oh Daddy, can't we give them lunch? They look so hungry and tired." Her father agreed, but Grandmother and my aunts were silently furious at little Queenie. Her penchant for "thinking in large terms" had gone too far. However, without a murmur, they set to work alongside household staff to set up picnic tables and produce lunch.

This silent disregard for herself was typical of my grandmother's attitude. Whatever her private feelings, she had a strong sense of duty and public service. She threw herself into her role as wife of a controversial mayor and mother of a growing brood composed of two step-children and eight children of her own.

R.J. was invited to become manager of the very Toronto Street Railway he had fought so hard against. He accepted this challenge. When the Twelfth of July came around and marching Orangemen began to create a ruckus, he had all the streetcars promptly stopped in their tracks. It didn't take long for things to calm down.

Grandmother Lydia travelled with him to England, where her capacity for friendship brought her many new friends. Among them was a Maharani from India, wife of a well-known Maharaja. She asked for Lydia's help to improve access to medical services for women in India. From then on, Lydia worked tirelessly to raise money in her own living room, in the homes of friends and at public events. She became an experienced storyteller in the process.

Meanwhile, Grandfather had more free time and enough money to go back to his first love, farming. In June of 1924 he had moved the whole family from St. Clair Avenue to Donlands farm, well beyond the city limits. Once again, their house in the growing city was no longer a place for cows. He had been holding a mortgage on Donlands farm. When the owner couldn't pay, he gave him a year's extension and then foreclosed. The owner's family hated him from then on. My mother decided she would never hold a mortgage.

Grandfather was interested in improving the quality of Canadian livestock. He made a number of trips to Scotland, Ireland, and the islands of Jersey and Guernsey to purchase the finest sheep, horses and cattle. From Scotland he brought out an older shepherd, Dick Hornby. Dick was a silent, reassuring presence around Donlands, as my grandmother's faithful, almost deaf handyman. The asparagus and tulip beds he planted grew better than anyone else's.

The youngest of the four Fleming daughters, Agnes, rode horses with a special flair. "There wasn't a horse she was afraid of," my mother would say. In their early twenties, Agnes and Murray lined the shelves of Donlands with silver trophies from Madison Square Gardens and the Royal Winter Fair. Two of the prizewinning horses they rode, Sharavogue and Deraney, were still at Donlands in the 1930s when I lived there. Grandfather enjoyed the trips to watch them and exchange information with other breeders.

In 1925, five years before I was born, Grandfather R.J. was helping the farm hands round up calves that had gotten loose while being driven aboard the freight train that stopped at the Don Mills Road cross-point. He caught a chill that developed into pleurisy and ended his life. In his bed at Donlands farm, his last words were, "Children, keep the family together. Love one another."

His funeral was one of the largest Toronto had seen. One editorialist wrote, "He never lost the common touch."

Being troubled about a couple of his sons and not knowing how to divide up his estate, he left no will. The prizewinning Jersey herd and the flock of sheep were sold to pay estate taxes. Toronto's first black alderman, William Peyton Hubbard, whose talent R.J. had spotted when he was a junior clerk, became advisor and a tower of strength to Grandmother and later her daughters. I knew him as Mr. Hubbard, a tall, open-hearted man who instilled confidence.

Portrait of Grandfather R. J. Fleming, taken while he was Mayor of Toronto. A painted portrait of him hung over the fireplace at Donlands, serenely presiding over the living room and used by his oldest daughters as a weapon to demand that the grandchildren live up to impossible standards.

Grandfather's portrait hung over the mantelpiece in the living room at Donlands. It dominated the whole room. He had a white moustache and eyes that looked straight at you. At his death, he weighed a portly 240 pounds. To my mother's annoyance, his idea of Saturday afternoon entertainment was to drive down to the farm at Whitby and talk cattle with his son Russell, while the women cooked a huge goose for supper. My mother had other ideas about how to spend a Saturday.

R.J. cast a large shadow for his sons to live under. He could be a stern taskmaster, forbidding his children ever to fight with each other, instructing them to keep quiet at table and to listen to their betters. There was little language in the family for sorting out differences. To me, he was something of a legend, hanging over the fireplace. Over the years it became tiresome to be told that our generation was supposed to live up to his achievements and messages. Under my breath I used to say "nuts" to Grandfather.

Fifty years later, my mother asked my husband and me what to do with the many volumes of Grandfather's public and private letters that she had hidden under a tarpaulin for years in the top floor of her cottage. They had been rescued from the 1940 fire at Donlands and stored by Aunt Stella. As I read these letters of a grandfather I had never met, I could approach R.J. without all the strictures and see him as a person who had genuinely suffered. His strength was in my genes and I could accept his story as part of my own. I donated the letters to the City of Toronto Archives.

After her husband's death, Grandmother Lydia decided it was time she went to see for herself the medical work in India that she had been helping to fund. The Maharani invited her to be her guest. She took with her two of her daughters, Evelyn and Agnes, whom she felt were far too caught up in the flapper lifestyle of the 1920s.

Aunt Evelyn was a young medical student, one of the few women to graduate in 1926. India appalled her. The poverty she saw just outside the gates of the Maharani's palace upset her profoundly. She couldn't sleep and the climate made her ill. A photo shows her sitting miserably in a tent, almost immobilized by a severe attack of rheumatoid arthritis.

With a sigh of relief, Evelyn returned to London to continue her medical studies. She was received at court, sailing in on the arm of Jamal, the darkly handsome son of a Middle Eastern aristocrat. She wore a silvery silk dress with a train and three ostrich feathers in a band around her head.

A few days later, she was strolling down along the side of Hyde Park, just down the road from the Dorchester Hotel where she loved to go for high tea. Suddenly, a feeling of great warmth and light came over her. She knew with complete certainty that she was to go back to India as a doctor. Within a few years, she became chief surgeon at a hospital in Northern India serving a million people. Through strict attention to diet, including regular juice fasting, she overcame her arthritis and it never returned.

Aunt Ev (left), ca. 1937, found a little girl with gangrene who had been left to die. Ev amputated the leg and saved her life. With Indian nurse on right, at the hospital south of Darjeeling.

She sewed up farmers who had been attacked by tigers. Sight was restored to many through eye surgery she learned during visits from a British specialist, Sir Henry Holland.

Aunt Ev's daily life in India became an integral part of life at Donlands through the letters and photographs she sent back. I remember particularly a photo of a young girl my own age who had been left to die of gangrene. Aunt Ev removed her left leg at the knee, gave her crutches and became her friend. In a letter, she described picking up a filthy bundle of rags that hid a little boy of eight. She carried him into the hospital and nursed him back to life.

"My greatest fear became my greatest joy," she told me. Some of her letters home revealed the homesickness of a young woman far away from her family. Living conditions in her first years were difficult. On her rare visits home to Donlands, none of this was mentioned. Stories of the beauty of India and its people, the dedicated young Indian nurses at the hospital, and a parade of colourful personalities expanded the walls of that living room.

Later, during World War II, Aunt Ev donned a uniform and returned from furlough on a troop ship, running with no lights and too few lifeboats through submarine-infested waters. Nothing could keep her away from India. By 1936, her mother had developed a heart murmur. The doctor advised Lydia to live a normal life, while her daughters tried to protect her, keeping the house as quiet as they could with all the comings and goings. In 1937, Grandmother ignored their protests and set off for India once again to visit Aunt Ev. Once again, she inspected the hospital, talking to the patients and asking questions with great interest. She was becoming something of a local celebrity in India.

LAKE SIMCOE

Some of my happiest and most nourishing childhood memories are of summers spent at my grandmother's cottage at Lake Simcoe. My mother shared with me her memory of travelling with her father, R. J. Fleming, all around the lake looking for a suitable vacation property to buy. Finally he found a farm off the 10th concession of Innisfil, a few miles from Stroud and south of Barrie, Ontario. His son, Goldie, had the first cottage built for my grandmother. She named it Goldwynden, after her son.

My earliest memory of Lake Simcoe was of being driven up to that cottage from Donlands with my mother by her brother Lloyd in the jaunty two-seater Hupmobile with a rumble seat. I was five years old. It was late on a summer evening when we left, and I fell asleep in the car. The next morning I woke up to the sound of water lapping on the shore. Magical. Days were spent pottering down to the sandy beach with pail and shovel, standing up to my knees in the warm, sun-speckled water, feeling the tiny fishes nibbling my toes as I hung onto the old wooden dock, or running across the lawn under the pine trees while my granny sat serenely rocking in her chair.

When other cousins arrived, a long table for children was set up on the screened porch. I celebrated my sixth birthday that September, and was given my first tiny bottle of perfume as I sat wriggling happily at the head of the table, scratching the odd mosquito bite. As a special treat we might even have toasted marshmallows, sitting around a big bonfire down on the shore.

Of course there were no refrigerators in those days. Instead there was a wooden icebox. The ice was cut in earliest spring from far out in the lake, then stored in the grey wooden icehouse back of the cottage.

Heat for the living room was provided by a wood-burning fireplace with a big iron mesh screen in front. Every evening during supper and in the living room afterward, we set aside the screen to enjoy the heat and the beauty of the fire.

I remember my mother driving me from Lake Simcoe to the Toronto Exhibition with my cousins from the farm at Pickering, Ontario. These five were the children of my Uncle

Russell and Aunt Doris. My mother wore a hat with a very tall feather on it that stood straight up so we could always find her. She wanted us children to expand our horizons. We were allowed to wander through as much of the grounds as we could manage, with the understanding that we would meet at a certain hour for the return trip.

One Sunday at Granny's cottage, in 1937, we had just finished noon dinner when we heard a strange crackling from upstairs, along with the sound of small objects dropping on the floor as though squirrels were throwing acorns.

Bob and Lou went up to investigate and I followed after them. Lou was first down the hall. Then he pelted back towards us yelling, "Fire, fire!" The three of us ran down the stairs, yelling "fire, fire" all the way. One of the grownups grabbed a phone and called the fire department. Someone else must have called Uncle Goldie and Aunt Jean, living in their own cottage on the other side of Mom's cottage, Peribonka.

The fire truck from Barrie arrived after some delay, but their hoses proved too short to bring water from the lake to the house. Aunt Jean climbed onto the roof with pails of water, but the wooden roof burned relentlessly. At one point, two of the pine trees caught fire, a truly horrifying sight. At this moment, the younger cousins and I were hurried off to Uncle Goldie's, where I remember sitting down to a second Sunday dinner, dazed and in shock.

Later, the only positive thing we could think of was that our darling Granny would never know of the fire at her cottage. That summer of 1937, she had gone back to India for a third visit, had fallen ill, and had died in Aunt Evelyn's arms. We were thankful that she didn't have to know about this loss. We were all gathered at my mother's cottage, Peribonka, when the cable arrived, announcing Granny's death. It was a moment out of time, when we came together as a family absorbing the shock.

Aunt Evelyn later told me that when she saw her mother's coffin being lowered into the hold of a Cunard ship for the long trip returning to Canada, it was the darkest moment of her life. Then she heard a quiet voice beside her. It was the ship's captain, saying, "Remember this is not your mother's body. She now has a risen, glorified body."

1937 was a sad Christmas back at Donlands. I remember huddling with the women of the house, for once treated as an adult, and the quiet sound of weeping. There was no Christmas tree and no presents. We waited while the ship made its way slowly through the Strait of Gibraltar. Uncle Lloyd boarded the ship there for one of his rare visits back to Donlands.

That casket came to rest in the living room at Donlands where it was piled high with flowers before being taken to Mount Pleasant Cemetery in Toronto. I remember taking a single rose and placing it among the other flowers. I learned from my grandmother to love, to commit and never to look back, whatever the circumstances.

I was seven years old and so glad to see Uncle Lloyd during that rare visit. He had won my admiration on an earlier visit by blowing smoke rings out of his ears. Years later, when my mother and I visited him at his home in Spain, my affection and respect for him deepened. I met some of the people he had been able to help through his own struggle with alcohol. He had founded Alcoholics Anonymous in Spain.

Another vivid personality who was briefly part of the household was Aunt Stella's husband, Murdoch MacKenzie. He had grown up in Scotland on a regime of porridge and a fourteen-mile walk to school. For thirty years, he travelled on foot as a missionary from village to village in China. Eventually, he became founding Moderator of the Presbyterian Church in

China. His first wife died there. He was thirty years older than Aunt Stella when he asked her to marry him and go back with him to China. It took her seven years to make up her mind, much to my mother's exasperation. Mother made up her mind rapidly, and rarely hedged thereafter. But Aunt Stella knew all too well from the letters of her friend Rosalind Goforth what conditions would be like. Rosalind had lost three children to dysentery and malaria.

In the end, Aunt Stella spent nine years in China, and grew to love the country. Then she brought Uncle Murdoch back to Donlands. His health had failed but his spirit had not. He brought with him a large carton of great books of the world which he had buried deep in the earth during the Boxer Rebellion of 1899 – 1901 in China. I spent magical hours listening to Aunt Stella read aloud from those books and others. I remember her reading with excitement about the discovery of insulin by the Canadian physician Frederick Banting and medical student Charles H. Best, who discovered the hormone in the pancreatic extracts of dogs. On July 30, 1921, they injected the hormone into a diabetic dog and found that it effectively lowered the dog's blood glucose levels to normal. The subliminal theme of both the book and Uncle Murdoch's stories of China was, "Don't give up, no matter what."

On Saturday afternoons, the stories of *Tristan and Isolde*, *La Bohème* and *La Traviata* would billow into the living room through the brown bell-shaped radio. There was never a dull moment with these characters. The mellow tones of Milton Cross, the radio host, kept us posted on what was happening during the Saturday afternoon Metropolitan opera broadcast.

Another character who suddenly appeared on centre stage at Donlands was Uncle Murray. A debonair man about town, he had just been divorced by his wife. He added a great deal of colour to our gatherings and was very meticulous. "Girls!" he would bellow to his sisters. "Who left these newspapers lying about?" At night I would creep down the stairs to listen to the gravelly voices of Amos and Andy, which he turned on during supper to drown out what he called "the religious twitter" of his older sisters.

Every day, Uncle Murray methodically brushed his hair 100 strokes so it wouldn't fall out. I spent hours happily pottering along in his company, helping him to inspect his race horses in the back barn. I loved offering a lump of sugar under the velvet snuffling of the colts, or lingering in the tack room with its smell of highly polished leather, or listening in on endless conferences with the head groom. Sharavogue, a show-stopping Irish jumper, was the star of the back stable. Occasionally, I was given a lift up to the dizzying height of his back after I eagerly promised not to tell my mother.

Of course, one of the great joys of those years was the occasional visit from my energetic cousin Lydia who lived in Montreal. Her parents travelled a lot but for long periods of time they lived in Montreal with the Hallward family.

One day when I was four and Lydia was three, the front door of the living room burst open and there were two identical curly-haired boys. Our twin cousins, Bob and Lou, had arrived. They were about five years older than me and immediately displayed their superior building skills. To our great delight, Tinker Toys appeared like magic all over the carpet of our grandmother's well-ordered living room. A tall windmill appeared before you could say jackrabbit. On that same visit, the doorbell started ringing madly in the middle of the night. No one could get it to stop. Lou had rigged the wiring. Dangerous chemical experiments now took place in the room in the attic formerly devoted to ironing. Bob was close to blowing us all to smithereens.

Sometimes five of the cousins would arrive from Pickering, Ontario, to join in the fun, children of Uncle Russell and Aunt Doris. One day, Bob and Lou dragged out the old horse-drawn sleigh from the barn and brought it across the fields to the steepest hill. With a mighty push, the sleigh was sent hurtling downhill to a narrow gap between two fence posts, with all of us on board, legs dangling out either side. Cousin Everett shouted, "We're going to be killed!" Fortunately, the sleigh shot straight through the gap without mishap. None of us breathed a word to the adults.

It was always a delight in summer when Aunt Doris arrived with the five Pickering cousins in tow. She used to cook their meals over an open fire near the icehouse, behind Granny's cottage, where they camped out for the summer.

One time Aunt Doris was frying sausages. The smell was intoxicating. Jumping the queue, my cheeky six-year-old self demanded, "Three sausages, please." I was never allowed to live it down. "Three sausages, please," was repeated at my 80th birthday celebration.

One summer day, my twin cousins invited me to join them for a paddle in my dad's Peterborough canoe. Eagerly, I accepted the offer. The boys paddled out to Uncle Goldie's raft, a fair distance from shore. They invited me to be first onto the raft. Then they paddled furiously away, leaving me stranded.

Granny Bentley had been watching from the shore. Now she jumped up and down in fury, shouting, "You dreadful boys, bring her back immediately," holding her green umbrella over her head to protect against the sun.

I enjoyed the whole adventure immensely. I sat down on the raft and pretended I was Huckleberry Finn, sailing down the Mississippi. Eventually Bob and Lou paddled back to rescue me, to the relief of the grown-ups gathered on the shore.

Another time, the boys dug a cave deep under the earth behind Granny's cottage. We younger ones ventured down there once or twice. Fortunately none of us were in the underground cabin when the rain-softened roof collapsed.

Occasionally, I would write short skits for my cousins to perform in front of long-suffering grown-ups. My first effort went down in history. After Sunday lunch the grown-ups were duly assembled. The play was entitled *Murder when the Clock Strikes Thirteen.*

We struck a gong once, twice, and up to twelve times. "The clock didn't strike thirteen," I announced, "so there will be no murder." The appreciative audience applauded and shouted, "Author, author!" Now the sleepy grown-ups, vastly relieved, were able to head for their after-dinner nap, and I was praised for my creativity.

To my dismay, these cousins all had a way of suddenly vanishing. Bob and Lou were sent off to a strict boarding-school by Grandmother when a football knocked down her ivory elephants. Lydia disappeared to Jamaica with her parents, sending back postcards of donkeys and palm trees.

One day, an ambulance arrived at Donlands with a polio-stricken Bob in it. It was the height of an epidemic that closed most of the schools, including my own. I was immensely pleased with this new development. Here was a cousin who would finally stay put. To occupy his active mind in my mother's room where he was ensconced, he was given the gift of a multiplying family of white mice.

With all this coming and going, my mother remained a warm and stable presence. A rebel herself, she did her best to mitigate the Victorian rules of the house. She obeyed Uncle Murray's injunction to appear properly dressed promptly at seven o'clock for dinner. There was no time to read me a bedtime story. But when the maid, Bella, changed the plates, my mother slipped upstairs to kiss me goodnight, dressed in her long green velvet dress, smelling of spinach and roast beef. When I let a flowerpot full of earth and geraniums roll down the front stairs just to see what would happen, she could hardly hide her laughter. I am still amazed at the freedom she allowed me to wander on my own over the front part of the farm, including the barn, the plowed fields, and Granny's garden.

In the big kitchen at Donlands, Aunt Stella would join Mrs. Gates, the cook, to pickle beets. Until the advent of pasteurization, Aunt Reba churned butter by hand from the fresh milk brought over each day from the barn. My mother won prizes for her bread at the Toronto Exhibition. I loved to hang out in the big kitchen where a soup pot always simmered away on the big wood stove. Mrs. Gates was often crotchety but she tolerated my presence in the kitchen. When I asked her what dessert was going to be, it was always "wait-and-see pudding." Too often, that meant tapioca pudding. Even my aunts failed to budge her rigid idea of a varied menu. White, grandmother's chauffeur, would often drop by to wheedle a cup of tea and liven things up.

Before school days began, the task of bringing up this exuberant child into line fell mainly to Aunt Reba. Aunt Reba had already helped her step-mother raise eight children, including my mother. She must have thought it was the last straw to have yet another energetic child land on her doorstep just when she was concerned about Grandmother's health.

One day when I was a preschooler, I lingered in the kitchen after I'd been ordered upstairs for my afternoon nap. I stayed behind to help the cook, Mrs. Gates, wash the dishes. We were chatting away when I heard the voice of Aunt Reba approaching from the far end of the hall. I dashed and managed to slip up the stairs unseen. I was just tugging my undershirt over my head when I heard her footsteps coming up the stairs. I grabbed a pair of scissors and cut the shoulder straps, then tried to hide under the covers, scissors, debris and all.

Aunt Reba had eyes in the back of her head. In silent fury, she hauled me along the hall to her room, insisted I kneel down at her footstool and ask God for forgiveness for being such a wicked, disobedient child. She informed me that God could see everything I did, and would punish me for the slightest infraction. I was just four years old.

I didn't disbelieve her. I was terrified. It was the beginning of a period of self-blame and self-doubt that would reappear over many years. In my twenties, I had a dream in which Aunt Reba and Aunt Stella said to me, "We didn't mean to stop you from laughing." I was able to let go the childhood hurt.

But because of that early incident, I added God to my list of formidable grown-ups to be steered clear of whenever possible. I didn't disbelieve in His existence, but I was underwhelmed by His way of going about things.

As soon as I got out of doors, all the injunctions were forgotten. It was as though the music inside me turned on again. Recently I came across James Hillman's *The Soul's Code.* In it he quarrels with modern psychology's attempt to explain our lives only in terms of early traumas or the effect of our families. He points to other influences, including the highly individual destiny or acorn pattern imbedded in each of us from birth. We need to pay attention to this pattern and the way it surfaces throughout our lives.

BISHOP STRACHAN SCHOOL

Granny arranged for me to enter kindergarten at the excellent Anglican girls' school, Bishop Strachan. Her chauffeur, Thomas White, would drive me the eleven miles to school Monday to Friday. Just for fun, he would drive the yellow Hupmobile to the top of the steep slope on Don Mills Road, leading down to the yellow brick bridge across the Don River. Then he would turn off the motor to see how far we could coast down the hill, over the bridge and up the other side.

Kindergarten was a whole new experience. Every day I was surrounded by a roomful of children. Thanks to Mum, I could already read. The teaching was relaxed under the supervision of Miss O'Rourke from England and I made some lifelong friends. In Junior One, the next year, we got a superb grounding in French from Madame Allen, for which I will always be grateful.

One of the special moments of that year was the invitation to be the youngest shepherd in the nativity play that Christmas. The audience sat in enthralled silence as the sacred story unfolded.

One warm summer evening when I was eight years old, I was hanging out of the one window of my small bedroom at the top of the front stairs. The grown-ups were all at dinner. The smell of the petunia bed was so strong I can almost smell it as I write. Just across from me on the far side of the gravel driveway was a huge Siberian elm tree. I was told that a tree like this might produce as many as two million leaves in a season. That sounds like a tall tale but nothing about that tree would surprise me. For over an hour on that summer evening I hung there communing with the tree, watching the early stars come out, listening to the cicadas and a whole bunch of insects whose names I didn't know carrying on in the grass.

Something wonderful was going on around me, a magnificent story that I belonged in, so powerful that I knew I had to try to find out somewhere, somehow, what the story was and how I could live out of it. I felt my consciousness expanding up, up to the stars and beyond, and I knew with complete certainty that I was held and I was loved.

While I was growing up, my mother told me stories about "Holy Ann," as she was known. Mum remembered seeing her sitting out in the sun when she herself was only eight years old. "Holy Ann" was born Ann Preston in 1810 on a farm at Ballamacally in Ireland. After a week in school, the teacher gave up trying to teach her the alphabet, tapped her on the forehead and said, "Poor Ann! She can never learn anything." She was taken out of school and put to herding cows and minding children.

She ended up working for Dr. Reid and his wife, who had seven children. Eventually he decided to move the family to Canada, to a small farm in Thornhill, north of Toronto, where his wife later died. Ann cared faithfully for the children. Unfortunately she would explode with temper whenever one of the children did something that annoyed her. Through the Methodist Church of her employer she discovered the power of prayer, and that miraculously she could decipher the words of the Bible. She began to pray about everything. "Father, where did I put that laundry?" or "Father, help me through the day today." Her temper tantrums disappeared. She was led into a new and joyful life.

The small well on the farm was always dry for several months in the summer. This meant the sons had to walk half a mile to fetch water for the family and the livestock. One day when Ann was talking to the children about a prayer-answering God, Henry Reid teased her with, "Ann, why don't you ask your Father to send water in that well and not have us boys work so hard?"

Alone that night, she prayed for water and added, "Father, you heard what Henry said tonight. If I get up in the class-meeting and quote the verse, 'My God shall supply all your needs according to his riches in glory by Jesus Christ,' and you haven't sent water to that well, they'll never believe a word again." She continued to pray, received an assurance, and fell asleep.

The next morning, Henry was getting ready for his long, strenuous walk, when he saw Ann pick up two empty pails and head for the well he had called "as dry as the kitchen floor." To his astonishment, she came back to the house with the buckets filled to the brim with clear water. All he could manage to blurt out was, "Why didn't you do that long ago and save us all that work?" Years later, a friend of Ann's who knew the truth of the incident said that from that time on the well was never dry again, even in the hottest summer.

After some time she became ill. The doctor told her she needed eggs and milk if she were to regain her strength. It was mid-winter and there were no eggs in the entire village. She began to pray for eggs. The next day a small white hen arrived at her front door, came in and went hopping up the short flight of stairs to the landing. Then it disappeared. Painfully she hoisted herself up the stairs. The little hen had laid a single egg in a small box on the landing. It did the same thing every morning for three months. Then the doctor told her he was now prescribing beef tea instead of eggs and milk. The little hen laid one last egg, gave a brief cackle, and was never seen again.

Soon neighbours began flocking to her side to receive prayers and healing. When she died at the age of 96, countless friends gathered at her funeral along with clergy of six denominations.

Clergy across the province spoke of her in their churches. The Mayor of Toronto said, "This week I had two honours. I met with the President of the USA and I was pall-bearer to

Holy Ann. I regard the latter as the greater honour." The life of Ann Preston was recorded in a book by Helen E. Bingham of Toronto entitled *An Irish Saint*. When I was last in Toronto I discovered that the small farm in Thornhill had been turned into a museum recognised by the Ontario Historical Society, with a plaque and shrine commemorating Holy Ann. She was buried in Mount Pleasant Cemetery.

In January 1940, when I was ten years old, a couple driving along Don Mills Road noticed flames coming from the roof of a house. They arrived at the front door of Donlands shouting, "Your house is on fire! Your house is on fire!" All the adults were gathered in the living room after dinner. I heard the shouts from upstairs in my room, and someone shouting, "The child, the child!" Aunt Margie, a cousin of my mother's who was staying with us came quietly up the stairs, helped me to put on winter leggings and a warm coat, pick up my teddy bear and a battered old doll and, with no sign of panic, walk quietly down the stairs and out into the night.

For the next hour I stood in the snow, holding my hysterical Airedale dog by the collar to keep her from rushing back into the house. With a great crash of glass an upstairs window fell outwards and there was my mother throwing out pillows and blankets. A fireman shouted at her to get her photos and her letters. She was too dazed to hear him, and all my father's letters were lost. They had been stored in a trunk in the attic. Downstairs, farmhands unscrewed the legs of my grandmother's piano and carried it out into the snow beside the mahogany dining room table. The chairs stood lopsidedly around it in a caricature of a dinner party. Finally Uncle Murray took me over to the boarding house where the foreman Angus McNab and his wife lived. Someone gave me a raisin tart. For years after I could not eat raisin tarts without feeling sick. My whole world had gone up in flames.

When I look back at that evening I can see it as one of the defining moments in my life. At the time it seemed like a catastrophe, the loss of my home, the loss of a way of life. Now I realize that we were all fortunate to have escaped unharmed. That event allowed me to begin to understand others whose losses in war were far more terrible.

My mother and I moved into a city apartment building with a smokestack that belched soot in through our windows. The small bedroom I shared with two students from the Toronto Bible School, Myra and Margaret, looked out on a brick wall. On rare visits back to the farm, I saw my dog. She had gone wild and eventually had to be put down.

I had no words to talk about what had happened. In our family at that time, troubles were not talked about. You simply went through them. That's exactly what my mother did. She was a fighter and set out to create a new life for both of us. Years later someone said to me, "You were lucky she did not become depressed." Indeed I was. She threw herself into the Opera Guild, the Symphony, the Girl Guides, and a book club. She arranged music lessons for me and the next Christmas a Pomeranian puppy appeared under the Christmas tree, so small it could sit in my hand.

My mother's qualities as a fighter and my stubbornness led to friction. I begged her to let me change schools. My mother loved the beauty of Bishop Strachan with its Anglican chapel and stone buildings. She got on well with the headmistress. I desperately wanted to go to a public high school so that I could meet boys. The answer was no, and there was no discussion. We had no common language to discuss issues or the feelings around them. My own anger turned inward.

Often I arrived late for school, when all the other girls had gone in to chapel. One day, I slipped into the principal's office, opened the lost-and-found drawer in a desk, snaffled a purse full of coins, put on my white veil and slid into my seat in the chapel. For a brief moment, I felt a respite from my profound inner sense of neediness. On another foray, I discovered how to pry a wallet loose from the locker of the wealthiest girl in the class. In daylight, I thought of it as an adventure. At night, I woke up in a cold sweat. I felt cut off from all my classmates. As I walked down the street, I searched for fallen coins and bus tickets. A preoccupation with money had taken hold of my life.

Catharine wanted to go to public school so she could meet boys.

Then several things happened. One evening my cousin Margaret Fleming invited me to come with her for a walk through the woods and fields behind Peribonka. She stopped for a moment in the middle of one of the fields.

As we stood silently, she said quietly, "Look up, Catharine." Sure enough, there were those same stars twinkling serenely in the night sky. She didn't say another word. No questions, no advice, just an experience of unconditional love. That cousin became a supportive older sister to me then, and later at Camp Tanamakoon in Algonquin Park where I was a camper, and she a highly respected counsellor.

The following year, a genuine friendship developed between Margaret's younger sister, Barbara, and me. She and her whole family lived just across the road from Mum and me in a huge house where I loved to go. Barbara and I hung semaphore signals in our windows to communicate with each other. At school, I began to rediscover my earlier love of learning for its own sake. Classes in Latin and French were stimulating. There were only six of us in the German class and we raced ahead.

After school, I practiced for a language scholarship exam with the help of an old hand-cranked gramophone. When the oral exam time came, a teacher whispered, "Why is this girl speaking with such a dram-at-ische Akzent?" I had been turning the handle of the gramophone too slowly. Nevertheless, I won several scholarships and was finalist for Governor General's Medal in Grade 13.

After school, there was also basketball. I loved the exhilaration of moving down the court at full speed in complete sync with my teammates, everything else forgotten. I learned that if I crashed into an opponent, the team would suffer a penalty. If I were blocked, I could simply step back a pace, throw the ball to a teammate and go looking for an empty space within goal range, an approach I've found valuable in groups ever since.

One day a teacher called me aside after class. She said to me, "I realize that you are dealing with some difficulties in your life. But there are one or two in your class who are worse off. Perhaps you can look around a little."

It was like a door being opened out of the intense self-absorption I had fallen into. I noticed one of my classmates, in particular, was closing in on herself. I reached out and we became friends. I was glad that we were able to give each other some companionship. Much later when our lives took us in different directions, I learned she had committed suicide.

During my teenage years, no matter how hard I tried, I felt I could never live up to my mother's expectations. She was so fast and so decisive, I simply froze around her. If I were washing dishes at my own pace, no doubt daydreaming, she would come up behind me and say, "Hurry up." Those quiet evenings together disappeared and I could feel a cloud of depression descending.

By now, my mum had bought a house down the road from the school. When I came home after school, the Warren Road house was often empty as she pursued her own interests. Left on my own, I would turn on the gramophone or the radio and dance around the house. Or I would go for long walks along St. Clair Avenue and look longingly in shop windows. I had no money but I could look.

During a school holiday, I went with my cousin Lydia to see a play put on by a group of teenagers called *The Drugstore Revolution.* Something in that play caught my attention and at that moment I decided to give back the money I had stolen and look for a new focus in my life. At the start of my final year, I walked into the principal's office and returned to her the money I had stolen four years earlier. I did the same with the girl whose wallet I had taken. It was only much later that I found the words to tell my closest classmates. But there was a sense of a new beginning.

In 1946, when I was sixteen, my mother bought a new car. Gas rationing had just ended after the war. She decided to drive us across the country to attend the Banff summer school in the Canadian Rockies. She wanted me to see our continent before I travelled elsewhere, as she guessed I surely would.

The Canadian roads west of the Great Lakes were sparsely travelled and pretty rough in parts. So Mum drove south across the American border. Our most memorable stop was at Yellowstone National Park. I remember with awe the power of Old Faithful, the geyser shooting steam eighteen feet in the air, and the pools of bubbling mud formed by acidic chemicals in the water that dissolved the surrounding rock.

I marvelled at the amazing array of creatures that made the Park their home. Few Canadians of my age had ever seen a bison or a big-horn sheep. I had seen moose before, but here they roamed freely in a landscape of exceptional beauty, the world's first National Park. There was a waterfall higher than Niagara and a wide canyon of a depth that took my breath away. The range of landscape and animal life was a fresh revelation to me of the wonder of creation.

VICTORIA COLLEGE

Freshman year at Victoria College at the University of Toronto was sheer delight. I stayed in residence with young women from towns all over Ontario. I joined the Debating Parliament and the chorus of *Ruddigore*, a Gilbert and Sullivan operetta. We were trained by a former director of the Doyly Carte Company in London. Our soloists were superb and the conductor, Godfrey Ridout, pushed and cajoled a good performance out of us. That year, I joined the crowd of students pouring down Bay Street behind our winning football team to plant the goalposts on the steps of City Hall.

I looked in on the various Christian groups on campus, but decided they were far too staid. At a rally conducted by a visiting Anglican priest from Britain who spoke extremely well, I decided firmly not to give my life to Christ. In Philosophy 1A,

I had learned that even the existence of God could be a matter of some doubt. Descarte's "I think, therefore I am" was a great relief. A whole inner structure of beliefs came crashing down.

Much more fun were fraternity parties, football games, and dates over coffee at Murray's Restaurant with idealistic discussions about life.

Five days before I was to enter the Modern Languages Honours course, two friends had advised me separately to switch to Honours English where the teaching was superb. It was good advice. For four years, I experienced a degree of excellence in thought and learning with Northrop Frye that I had not known existed. Immersed in 700 years of English Literature, I kept asking myself, "Where do you find the way into the mystery of the elm tree? How could you live today in a way that would match the magnificence of the landscape you had known as a child?" Answers escaped me.

In my second year, under pressure from my mother, I broke off a year-long relationship with a boy I had fallen in love with. It was a difficult and painful decision. As soon as I had made the decision, an inner image rose up that was so powerful it took over my mind for the next few days. I found myself alone in the middle of a vast desert with a mountain rising up out of it. Having turned down the Christians, I hadn't expected to find myself with Moses in the middle of the Jewish scriptures. But there it was. It was clear that I was to climb the mountain, but the symbolism perplexed me, and after a few days the image vanished.

I dated another student and eventually ended up wearing his fraternity pin. It was a carefree and happy time. I experienced a heady freedom from obligation. He eventually put an engagement ring made of seaweed on my finger as we walked along the beach at Peribonka. That, too, ended when I left for Europe after graduation.

In my third year, I took part in a closely-contested election for the post of College Representative to the National Federation of Canadian University Students. My opponent was one of the few professed communists on campus. Her parents had been missionaries in China.

I won the election but came out of it with an uneasy feeling that she was committed to

Catharine Turnbull at Victoria College, about age 19 (ca. 1950)

something beyond herself in a way I was not. I hadn't agreed with her ideas, but as I looked around Toronto in the fifties, I thought, "There has to be more to life than this." Montrealers would heartily agree with this assessment of Toronto, but that's not what I meant as a college student.

Europe 1950 – 1956

At the end of my second year at Victoria College, an invitation arrived to meet my Aunt Evelyn in Europe. She was buying a new car to ship back to India, and had a few weeks free to drive through Europe. My mother made all the arrangements for the car and off we sailed on a Cunard steamship.

We landed in Holland, where I was awestruck to meet Lotte Van Beuningen, a white-haired matriarch who had been head of the Dutch Red Cross. During the war she set herself the task of persuading six Nazi commandants, one after the other, to allow her to send food into a nearby concentration camp where the prisoners were starving. Lotte prayed for guidance before each encounter. The third commandant said brusquely to this dignified woman, "Meet me in the brothel." Without batting an eyelid, she did just that. Only the sixth one proved intractable, but by then the war was in its final phase.

For the next six weeks, we explored Holland, France, Monaco and Italy. My cousin Lydia was working as conference staff at a hotel up a mountain at Caux-sur-Montreux in Switzerland. I left the others and went to spend a few days with her.

© CAUX-Initiatives of Change
Mountain House, Caux-sur-Montreux, high above Lake Geneva, Switzerland

The mountain had materialised. It looked out on one of the more beautiful views in the world, down the length of Lake Geneva, with the snowy caps of the Mont Blanc range at eye level.

The elegant hotel had been occupied by refugees during the war who left it in shambles. At war's end, three Swiss families donated a considerable part of their private fortunes to turn the hotel into a centre for reconciliation. Former enemies were meeting there for the first time. A group of volunteers, including my friend Clare Hallward, had done a huge clean-up of the hotel before I joined the group.

Those first days at Caux-sur-Montreux made an indelible impression. There were over 1500 people at the hotel from all over Europe. There were dock workers and diplomats from Great Britain, leaders of international organizations, and Marxist trade union leaders from the Ruhr. That first week included a large number of Italian factory workers and their factory owners. The energy in the plenary sessions in the great domed hall was electric. Stories were being told whose depth and humanity were profoundly moving.

I had a chance to catch up with my cousin, Lydia. One day we had lunch with other students and a fiery trade unionist from the Ruhr, Max Bladeck. He and his Marxist comrades had fought in the underground against Hitler. One of his comrades, Willi Benedens, had been sent off to the Russian front where he lost a leg. Max told us that in this atomic age, the class war was outdated. He had learned to listen to a deep inner voice for a new direction in his life. He had gone back to his Catholic roots.

I wanted to stay in Europe then and there but my mother insisted that I finish university in Canada.

In 1952, I graduated with honours from Victoria College. It had been four packed years, crammed with reading from centuries of English literature, including Chaucer. I sat riveted at lectures by Northrop Frye, one of the century's leading literary theorists. I felt honoured that he and his wife had been kind enough to invite my class to their home. I read later in his notes about that evening, "Catharine Turnbull asked an interesting question." A nice compliment.

Those years were not, however, a good preparation for writing. They were intimidating because we read so many excellent writers. My husband Neil, on the other hand, was advised to study something he could write about, so he studied history. I have no regrets. The courses were stimulating and I made some good friends. I'm embarrassed to remember that some of us would meet for coffee at Murray's and then walk in late to Northop Frye's lecture. Of course he would stop lecturing until we were all seated, much to the annoyance of the rest of the class.

My mother had hoped I might become a teacher. But all I wanted by the end of four years was some action. I was especially bored by being asked to serve at my mother's tea parties where all the ladies arrived wearing ornate hats and talked about what seemed to me to be daily nothings. It was only much later that I realized they were coping as best they could with some pretty difficult situations.

When my Aunt Agnes invited me to go back to Europe with her husband Eric and daughter Lydia, I jumped at the chance. That summer I was astonished once again by the international conference for reconciliation at Caux, Switzerland. I saw the power of their vision for transformation in our world.

Delegates from all the European countries that had been at war had been invited to attend. I worked as a waitress in the large dining room with a magnificent view of the countryside. I ended up translating between the French and German students who were also serving in the dining room. My years at Bishop Strachan School had given me a good grounding in both languages.

I enjoyed the cool, clear air of the Swiss Alps high above Lake Geneva, and the fun of running the dining room with a group of international young people. It was hard work but the purity of the mountain air gave us energy. After our shift we climbed further up the mountain to a restaurant where we could get delicious cheese fondue. I remember the mountain goats that looked as though they had two shorter legs when they perched on the side of the mountain.

I had the privilege that summer of rooming with Princess Lucy of Bunyoro, daughter of the King of Bunyoro, a kingdom in Western Uganda. She was a sturdy young woman but someone had decided that royalty was not required to work as hard as the rest of us. It was my pleasure to introduce her to the other young people and to share laughter.

In the evening, it was theater time in the hotel. The work of reconciling countries that had been at war brought out a remarkable degree of creativity. Plays included The Forgotten Factor, The Good Road, Jotham Valley, The Man with the Key, and eventually The Vanishing Island. My Uncle Eric Bentley took part in several of them. And of course the International Chorus was on constant call, with its repertoire of songs and national anthems from around the world. I vividly remember the Prayer of St. Francis, sung by Bill Baumann. It had been put to music by Herbie Allen, a talented and soon-to-be-famous Californian who to my amazement later became a lifelong friend.

At one point during the summer, Aunt Agnes Bentley decided our family needed a holiday and we went for a week of blissful relaxation at a Swiss resort.

TRANSLATING IN SWITZERLAND

Refreshed after the holiday, I went back again to Caux in Switzerland. The second day, I was sitting on the side of the hall not far from the speaker's platform when a tall, aristocratic-looking German woman walked up the steps. There was a slight flurry nearby. She was going to speak in German, and the usual German-to-English translator was absent. Without thinking, I jumped to my feet and joined this woman on the platform. As she spoke, she used a vocabulary far beyond anything I had learned at school, and yet I knew exactly what she was saying and how to translate it. Her story went right through me and out to the audience. I could feel the energy in the whole room. Her name was Frau Moni von Cramon and she came from an aristocratic German family.

She had risked her life to try to convince the leadership of her country to stop the preparations for war. She and her family had been under constant surveillance by the Gestapo. Her son-in-law had taken part in the failed Operation Valkyrie against Hitler and had been strung up with piano wire with the other conspirators. She told of instances when listening to an inner voice had shown her the next step to take as she survived until the end of the war.

In the audience that day was a French woman named Irène Laure. She was the leader of three million French Socialist women. During the war she had led hunger marches through the streets of Marseilles protesting the actions of the Nazi regime. Her son had been tortured in front of her. He survived but her hatred of the Germans grew. When she heard German being spoken at Caux, she headed to her room to pack her bags. In the hallway she met someone who listened to her and quietly asked her one question, "How will you build a new Europe without the Germans?" She fought a bitter struggle within herself. Over lunch the next day, she and Moni von Cramon listened to each other's stories and wept.

The next day Irène Laure got up to speak, dressed in the simple black dress she always wore. In the audience was a tall, blond young German named Peter Petersen, a former member of the Hitler Youth. With his deep-set eyes and a chip on the shoulder, he looked the part. He had sworn to leave immediately with his whole youth group if one word was said against Germany.

Very simply, Irène told her story. She said, "I do not forget the past, but I ask the Germans present for forgiveness for my hatred of their whole people." There was complete silence in the hall for a time. Peter was stunned. For the next years, he would give all his time and energy to the building of a new Europe. Irène Laure travelled all over Germany, speaking in each of the State Parliaments, with the same message she had expressed that day. In Berlin, she wept as she watched women picking up rubble with their bare hands. "This is what hatred does."

With my own eyes I was seeing people finding their way through the darkness of war. I decided I would do anything to be part of this story. That autumn I stayed with the parents of the woman Peter Petersen later married. The Junkers had lost most of their savings in the aftermath of the Versailles Treaty. Herr Junker painstakingly corrected my German and teased me about my late arrival.

Former Hitler Youth, Peter Petersen, later active in European reconciliation politics, marries Ilse Junker, daughter of Catharine's first hosts in Germany.

I had blithely flung myself onto the train from Bonn to Leonberg with a few minutes to spare. When the conductor came to punch my ticket, he said to me, "You are on the right train but you are going in the wrong direction." Indeed I was. It was symbolic of a good deal of my life for the next few years. I stayed with another family north of Bonn and headed for Leonberg the next day.

Frau Junker taught me how to make spaetzle, a German pasta, in her charming Schwäbisch accent. I wandered around their tiny village into the butcher's shop which seemed to display a hundred kinds of wurst, then along to the blacksmith who was still using the old skills.

That winter I was invited to the home of the young violinist, Trude Spoun, who later became Director of the Stuttgart School of Music. Together we climbed inside the steeple to the top of the magnificent Ulm Cathedral. All around the foundation of the Cathedral was a huge, empty flat space where dozens of houses had once clustered. I heard about the relentless bombing when all those homes went up in flames. Trude's sister, Inge, lived not far away and had not been able to get to the hospital for the birth of her first baby. I remembered the houses burning over my head at Lake Simcoe and at Donlands, and understood that the difficult things we go through can allow us to connect more deeply with other people.

Later my mother came with me to visit that hospitable family in Ulm. She, Trude and I went for a memorable meal of Danube trout at a cosy restaurant.

Four Winters in the Ruhr

Years later, I had a long conversation with Trude. Over the phone from her home in Stuttgart, she described to me the whole background of the work we were part of, as she now understood it.

"Before the war, the communists had been working for years to infiltrate the miners. The plan was to take over the Ruhr, then the rest of the country. Germany was to be a

threshold for the takeover of Europe. Many of us were glad
to have Hitler come along because we knew communism was
taking hold and we were afraid. The Versailles Treaty had
destroyed our economy. We were left with debts running into
this century.

"We didn't know it at the time, but working with MRA,
we were part of history. The communists had their plan but
we were part of a cure. We created our century."

MRA stood for Moral Re-Armament, a movement
launched on the eve of war in 1939. Both the Caux centre
and other work in which I would be involved in Europe were
sponsored by MRA.

That winter I was invited to join an international group
of young people in the mining area of Germany. My job as
one of the volunteers was to help run Haus Goldschmieding,
a mansion that had been loaned by the mining company.
I remember walking from the train station to get to my
destination. The whole area around the station had been
bombed out and only weeds were growing there. It was a
desolate scene.

There were not many Canadian students travelling in
Europe so soon after the war. I found myself working with
former Norwegian and Danish resistance fighters at Haus
Goldschmieding. A senior member of the team was a Czech,
John Pribram, who had lost both his parents and his leg in
the war. I valued the friendship of these people a great deal,
and their courage in returning to the country of their former
enemy. There was an honesty in the group, which included
young Germans, and the camaraderie of working towards a
shift in the direction of history. I was unsure of my own role.
I had no dramatic story to tell and not much to say. I simply
worked hard at whatever needed doing. Once I climbed nearly
eighteen feet on a tall ladder to wash the walls and ceilings

of the huge house. Haus Goldschmieding was a place where miners and management could meet to hammer out a new partnership. Later this partnership was evaluated as a major factor in preventing the takeover of the whole of the Ruhr by Marxism.

I was also supposed to chip in with the cooking. John Pribram commented kindly if slightly sarcastically about my amateur efforts. In time, he became a supportive older brother when I felt most down and discouraged. Later he went to the U.S. and trained as a mediation counsellor. We kept in touch over the years and I learned a lot about mediation from him.

During those years in Europe, I spent every summer at Caux, often heading up a work team in one of the dining rooms. There I would translate German into French, with some garbled Italian thrown in as we rushed to make coffee for the stream of people arriving. It was hard work but we were rejuvenated by long hikes up the mountain through gentian-covered meadows where cow-bells tinkled steadily from the necks of the mountain cattle.

For part of one winter I travelled as a stagehand with the German cast of a play originally produced at Caux to express a new approach to diplomacy. We stayed with different families every few days, talking with them about a new Europe. My job was to find props for the play in every new town and to see that everything on stage was in its proper place.

After the play, we went out into the audience and talked until after midnight. I worked with the other stagehands to haul all the props up by rope to the only part of the great Stuttgart Opera House that was intact after the waves of bombing. I was good at my job but it was exhausting.

I also spent some time in England. One day I received a letter from my cousin, Margaret Fleming, saying she was arriving by plane two days later. I went out to meet her at the airport and immediately sensed that something was wrong. Over supper, she told me that she had become engaged to a fellow student whom she described in glowing terms. But when her father discovered he was Catholic, he told her if she married this young man, she would never set foot in his house again.

Margaret broke off the engagement but she didn't speak to her father for six months. I was troubled by how pale and listless Margaret seemed. The following week I was due to return to Caux for the summer and I persuaded her to come with me.

At Caux, Margaret met Juliet Rodd and several other young women. She was captivated by the vision, and in a moment of dedication, gave her life to Christ. She even took off the necklace containing small pearls she had been given each year since childhood, and handed it to Paul Campbell as her donation. He hesitated, reluctant to take it from her, but she insisted.

She wrote a long letter to her father, apologizing for her hatred. A few days later, he arrived with a rented car, bought her a lovely new coat, and told her things he had never talked about with anyone. Then he invited both of us for a short trip around Switzerland before saying good-bye.

Later she was posted to London, where she met King Michael of Romania in exile and his wife Anne. They became friends but the higher-ups reassigned Margaret to less exalted work as housekeeper. Her talents were never made use of and when I saw her later in the United States, she was feeling disillusioned and used. One night I was so exhausted that I asked her to help me set the table. She blew up at me. Then when she saw me moving down the big table, limping in pain, with tears spilling down my cheeks, she relented and came to help.

Months later, I got a letter from her. She was in Japan, looking after the children of an MRA couple while they were away. Could I send over a game of Monopoly? I did so gladly. She was also teaching English as a second language at the university and was in her element. Good news indeed.

Then out of the blue I got a phone call from Clare Hallward that shocked me so much I nearly fainted. Margaret had accidentally tripped and fallen over the back of a dining room chair. She spent a few days in bed, then had been taken

Cousin Margaret Fleming in her element teaching English in Japan before her untimely death in 1964 at age 34

to hospital at the insistence of Dr. Paul Campbell, who happened to be in Tokyo.

She died in the middle of the night of a blood clot. This was a huge loss to all of us who knew her. At her funeral in Toronto, the President of University College spoke movingly of her as the most gifted all-round student in his many years of experience.

As the years in Europe wore on, my inner questions intensified. There seemed to be no time to stop and assess where I was going. I often felt out of my depth. An inner desolation was reappearing. Increasingly I waited to respond to what senior members of the group thought I should do next. There were few moments when I experienced the sense of elation I had known during the first days at Caux. I translated in public as seldom as possible to avoid the sharp criticism that could descend on anyone, and especially on any woman, who had a high profile on the full-time team. A friend said to me, "You seem to have put your personality on the shelf." It was clear that I had lost a sense of responsibility for my life and actions.

Later I found a description of this state in a book called, *The Wrong Way Home*. Its author, psychiatrist Arthur Deikman, outlined ways of thinking that allow people to be manipulated by a surprising number of organizations to which they belong. He called it the desire deep in all of us to sit in the back seat of a car—to be taken care of. It leads perfectly ordinary people to take part in cults.

It is embarrassing to see this behaviour in oneself, so we bury our awareness. My college friends had become all too aware that something had changed in me when I came back from Caux the first time, but they would not discuss it with me. Too quickly I had adopted the language and even the slogans of other people. I dropped out of the music club and most other college activities. I stopped wearing make-up. Since I was anaemic at the time, this gave me a suitably pale and dedicated look. I had the trappings of a True Believer.

The truth was that my new-found freedom at college had scared the hell out of me. I didn't know what to do with it beyond a certain point. The protective colouring of a group exerted a strong pull. I had found a Cause.

Much later when I read *The True Believer* by longshoreman philosopher, Eric Hoffer, I came to terms with this embarrassingly predictable behaviour. I also paid attention to its tendency to resurface. Hoffer's experience told him that "true belief" takes us a certain distance along the way we are seeking. It is not totally bad. But real growth occurs only when we go beyond.

For me there is no question that the post-war work of Caux made a significant contribution. I was there when Robert Schuman, Foreign Minister of France, arrived, asking, "Where are the Germans I can trust?" Together, he and Konrad Adenauer created a coal union, the foundation for the future European Union. There were too many outstanding people involved to be able to dismiss the work with a shrug. There were also some quite serious casualties, and a tendency to devalue outsiders. Whole books have been written evaluating both sides of this work.

My friend Trude Spoun reflected, "When I look back at all that was accomplished in the many countries I travelled to, the benefits of MRA far outweigh the negatives. I am also grateful for the friends around the world that are part of my life."

Much later I would find the experience of immense value in sorting out what works in groups and what does not. Some of my friends went on to make significant contributions in their own right. As I mentioned, John Pribram, my Czech friend from the Ruhr, worked as an effective arbitrator for the courts of Minnesota. Later he was named Arbitrator of the Year. I think church groups and sociology departments would find the study of the story of Caux both inspiring and cautionary.

When any one group or individual claims to have snaffled a monopoly on wisdom, it is time to watch out. And as I had found at my cost, it is important to have a good grasp on one's own story.

The name Moral Re-Armament has since been changed to "Initiatives of Change" by a younger generation who didn't like the old name any better than I did. I've long since distanced myself both from the name and from the organisation, as have many of my friends. I was never happy about the criticism, especially of strong women, or the demand that volunteers like me live up to impossibly high standards of behaviour, working long hours without pay. Once a Danish girl and I were setting tables for four hundred people. We were literally running in order to finish the settings in time for lunch. One woman who had never spoken to me before, snapped, "Your problem is impurity." MRA supporters were supposed to measure themselves against four absolute moral standards: honesty, purity, unselfishness, and love. All I could think of was that, not knowing me, she said this because I was pretty. I was profoundly upset; what was I supposed to do?

Years later I met that critical woman, Emmy Pyer, when I went to Taizé in France for a week. How different the conversation was. She told me she had been criticized so harshly that she nearly committed suicide. Yet she and her husband were one of the three couples who had given their entire fortunes to buy Caux. After leaving Caux, she and her husband met Brother Roger, a founder of Taizé. The meeting was transformative. Brother Roger talked freely with them about his own concerns in creating a monastic community. Emmy and Eric had found a new outlet for their creative energy.

After four years of winters in Germany and summers at Caux, I found the old patterns of depression returning. The contrast between the broad vision, the inspiring theater and a darker side of constant criticism from some senior members, as well as the control from the top, created some serious conflicts that I was unable to resolve in myself. My mother came to see me three times during those four years, when she thought I needed her. Those leisurely trips down through France to visit Uncle Lloyd in the south of Spain were a welcome time of relaxation.

By 1956, I was 25 and it was clearly time to head home. I was burnt out and full of self-doubt. I had tremendous gratitude for the friends I made and for the privilege of being exposed to a broader world, but there were also lessons learned about the dark side of groups and the suffering they can cause.

RETURN HOME

DETROIT AND FRIED CHICKEN

Returning to Canada from my volunteer work in Europe, I was exhausted, over-stimulated and had no sense of where my life was headed. I decided to travel via Detroit to visit Aunt Ella who had kept in touch with me over the years.

The first evening I went toward the phone to call my mother to say that I would be taking the train to Toronto the next morning. Something stopped me almost dead in my tracks. I couldn't pick up the phone. It was as if some force were almost physically holding me back. I turned around and went back to the kitchen where Aunt Ella was standing at the stove with her back to me, frying chicken for supper.

Aunt Ella was a short, stocky woman of eighty-one who had been a missionary in China. The bun of hair that curled on top of her head was still a warm brown. Every year she wrote six hundred letters to younger and older friends all over the world. When I was a girl at Donlands, she sent me a subscription not to a religious magazine but to *Child Life*. Her sister, Cora, had been married to my father and had died quite suddenly. Aunt Ella stayed in touch with my dad.

As she stood at the kitchen stove frying pieces of chicken, she began talking about my dad in a natural way that no other adult had been able to muster. She knew he had been killed in a car accident when Mum was four months pregnant with me.

Aunt Ella was able to hold the reality of life and death with a tranquility that was new to me. My mother had known Dad for little more than a year. To her he was an icon, the perfect husband that no one else would ever be able to match. It was a level of emotion I could not share. All I knew of my father was a rather distant, formal-looking photograph hanging on the bedroom wall.

"Your father was the kind of man everybody loved," she said. "He had an irrepressible sense of fun, and the kind of presence on a platform that could quiet a whole audience. He was known as the 'dress coat of the Alliance.'" The Alliance was the Christian Missionary Alliance, an ecumenical movement sponsored by several churches.

Aunt Ella told me the young man who had driven the car on the night of Dad's death had gone to Thailand where he had remained as a missionary ever since. He had just come back for a week's visit and was going to preach the following night in her Detroit church. Would I like to meet him? I hesitated for just a moment then said, "Of course."

The next night I stood in the pew as this man came toward me. I felt a great current of love and forgiveness running through me towards him. He said to me quite simply, "I wished it had been me. I wanted to die that night and many nights since. Your dad was my beloved teacher. It was your mother's faith that kept me going. She said to me, 'You have a life to live and you must live it.'" We talked for nearly an hour. He told me details about the accident I had never heard. "Your dad was to take the train home from New York to be with your mother in their new house. I was then a brash young guy with a brand new car. I offered to drive him. He accepted immediately and fell asleep in the back seat. There were no seat belts in those days.

"All went well as we travelled north along the Hudson River. I was feeling my oats. Then we turned a corner. A considerable pile of sand had drifted across the road. I gunned the car. It skidded into the ditch and the whole side of the car was smashed in. Your dad was thrown out and his temple hit the stone gatepost of a large house. He was killed instantly.

"People tell me it was a freak accident but I've blamed myself all these years." As the two of us sat there with tears welling up, the interior river of ice around the whole image of my dad melted. It was the first time I had been able to cry for the death of my father. I thought of the odds of meeting this man, all the way from Thailand for just one week. Me coming from Europe for just twenty-four hours to Detroit of all places. What were the odds? I never saw this student of Dad's again, but from then on, I knew at the core of my being that there was a Presence that I called a "You" at the heart of the universe that cared about ordinary, fragmented people like myself.

Later, my dad's nephew, Wally Turnbull, filled me in on more details about Dad. My dad's father, John Colclough Turnbull, was the owner of the general store in Peterborough, Ontario. He had six sons. He offered each of them the money for either a 100-acre farm or a college education. Three of them decided on a farm and did very well. The other three brothers, Walter, Louis and John decided on the college education.

Dad travelled to India, which was then a British colony, with his brothers Louis and John. There they founded churches and schools combined with orphanages. They did this in the midst of the 1920s famine.

The brothers would pray all night for food. In the morning, supplies would arrive, just enough for the most immediate needs. During the day, Dad would go around to the mill owners, smartly dressed and wearing his top hat, to ask for jobs for the orphans. My father and his brothers trained local leadership to carry on when the time came for them to return home.

Catharine's paternal grandfather, John Colclough Turnbull, age 35, offered each of his sons the money for a farm or a college education.

At some point during their stay in India, Dad married a fellow missionary. Together, they travelled the long, hot journey by sea back to Canada.

Soon afterward, she died in childbirth. Heartbroken, he buried his young wife in Mount Pleasant Cemetery in Toronto.

He started travelling to visit the CMA missions and to explore locations where others could be founded. He explored parts of Peru on foot and visited the Inca ruins of the stone cities on the edge of Lake Titicaca. He visited Cusco, the capital of the Inca empire, and climbed Macchu Picchu, 9000 feet above sea level, where the sun and moon came together to create the world. It was Peru's Garden of Eden with an intricate network of temples and gardens.

In the 1920s he helped found the Christian Missionary Alliance College in Nyack, New York on the Hudson River. His father provided some of the early financing. Their idea was not to impose on the students but to train them. A well-loved teacher and Dean of Men, known for his sense of humour, Dad used to enter into pillow fights with his students. I was told he sent more missionaries to foreign service than any man of his generation. His nephew Wally Turnbull later told me that clearly an immense amount of creativity and long-range thinking went into the creation of the College.

In the brief intervals between semesters, he travelled across Canada and the U.S., preaching in churches wherever he went. At some point in his career, he went to China. My mother told me that he also walked on foot in other Asian countries, visiting missions and looking for locations for new missions.

Well into his years at Nyack, Dad fell in love with and married a fellow teacher, Cora Rudy, sister of Aunt Ella. Their life together was a busy and happy one, with students constantly in and around their welcoming home. The frequent visits by their three young Turnbull nephews was a special joy. Dad loved children and hoped for one of his own. But it was not to be. Cora's death was pure heartbreak for Dad. His health suffered and it was a long time before he was fully back on schedule.

In early 1928, my grandmother decided that her middle daughter, Victoria, needed some guidance. Victoria was a rebel who wanted to wear bloomers on Sunday. She had wanted to go to university but her father decided that since her sister Stella hadn't done much with her college degree, Victoria would go to missionary college in Western Canada instead.

She returned home saying only that the food had been poor and the teachers uninspiring.

Next she persuaded her parents to let her spend two years with her sister Stella and her husband Murdoch MacKenzie in China, where she learned basic Mandarin. Now she was at loose ends.

Grandmother heard about a weekend seminar being preached by Dr. Turnbull in Nyack, New York. She decided she and Victoria would go. There were people from all over North America attending. As Dad preached, he noticed a young woman in the audience, listening intently. Back in his room, he got down on his knees and prayed, "Lord, give me a chance to meet this young woman or take her out of my mind." A few minutes later, there was a knock on the door. It was the young woman in question, Victoria Fleming. In her hand was a letter from my grandmother inviting him to come to Toronto to preach. It was the first of several such letters.

Grandmother had many contacts in Toronto. As a young woman she had played the piano in the Sackville Street inner city mission. Later she founded the Zenana Bible Mission. Dad managed to be in Toronto on many occasions. At the time, my mother couldn't understand why he accepted invitations to preach in Toronto so often. When he proposed to my mother, Grandmother was shocked. This famous man wanted to marry her rebel daughter?

Plans for the wedding were made very quickly and simply. No big church. It was to be in the living room at Donlands with close family and friends. No white gown for my mother, just a simple dress from a Toronto dress shop. Her sister, Evelyn, who had just become one of the first women in Toronto to graduate in medicine, would be her maid of honour.

Alexandrina Victoria Fleming and Walter Mason Turnbull
on their wedding day July 25, 1929

I learned more about this wedding of July 25, 1929 when
I at last got to see the original silent film of it at the age of
eighty-five, thanks to my friend Jean Plourde, who found the
film among the tapes of my husband's radio show. There is
my beloved mother smiling from beneath her Twenties cloche
hat, with Dad contentedly in attendance. What a gift for me
after all these years to finally see my dad as other people
saw him. There is Granny, chatting with her guests. Only
a few select friends were invited. There is Uncle Murdoch
MacKenzie, back on furlough from China, with his white hair

and beard welcoming the guests as they arrived in a wonderful assortment of Twenties vehicles, the women all wearing cloche hats and flapper dresses.

My mother told me she was a bundle of nerves during the wedding, but as soon as she was alone with Dad she relaxed. My parents went to Quebec on their honeymoon, to the Peribonka River which they travelled by canoe, then back to Nyack where Dad used all his money to buy a house on campus.

When Mum learned she was pregnant, Dad was overjoyed. He bought a little pair of booties and a small silk coat, both of them pink. Did he somehow intuit I was to be a girl?

Four months into her pregnancy, my mother went to bed, knowing Dad would be coming home on a late train. She was awakened by a gentle hand on her shoulder. The hand was shaking. It was my grandmother who told her the shocking news that Dad had been killed in a car accident. The following days were a blur.

Mother insisted that Dad be buried in the family plot in Toronto.

After the funeral she set about selling the new house they had just bought at Nyack. Dad had no pension and little money in the bank. She had no choice but to move back to Donlands to her mother and a bossy older sister. I was born in September 1930. Later, dapper Uncle Murray joined us after his divorce. When Uncle Murdoch became ill in China, Aunt Stella brought him back to Donlands for the rest of his days.

After my visit with Aunt Ella in Detroit, I spent a few months with my mother to recharge my batteries, then I joined my friends in Moral Re-Armament on Mackinac Island, Michigan.

The summer of 1956 was a busy one.

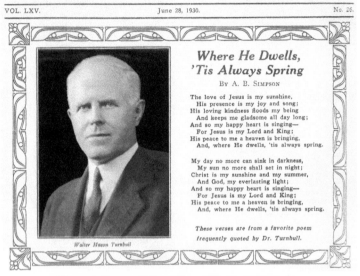

Memorial issue of *The Alliance Weekly* dedicated to
Catharine's father, Walter Turnbull

Victoria Fleming Turnbull with baby Catharine 1930

U.S.A. 1956

DELLWOOD

O ne day, one of the senior team members at Mackinac, Ellie Newton, came to see me. She told me her niece Robley Geddes needed help at an estate where she was housekeeper. Would I be willing to join her? At the time we younger people were not allowed off the island without permission. This restriction and others created a much less inspiring experience than Europe had been, so I jumped at the chance.

Dellwood turned out to be an impressive estate in the country, an hour north of New York. It had been donated for the work of Moral Re-Armament by Emily Hammond. A week after I arrived, Robley quit and went home for good. This left me on my own with the prestigious title of head housekeeper, scrubbing toilets and making beds as visitors came and went. Among the most memorable were a group of Japanese involved in reconciliation.

I was expected to serve supper around eight o'clock when the team came home from New York. When I gently suggested they serve themselves, I was scolded for my thoughtlessness. What saved my sanity was that Norah Considine invited me out every Saturday night for a good supper. She had been head housekeeper in Emily Hammond's time and saw what I was going through. Now we sat watching boxing matches on television while we ate, as she had done with her late husband.

Norah also invited me to drive to mass with her on Sundays. There was no question whether I would attend with her; I loved the Latin mass. I could just sit and relax my tired bones. Then one day at work, my hip that had been malformed at birth gave out completely and I ended up in bed for three days. The third day when I came down for supper, Betty Belk got up out of her seat and placed a hot plate of food in front of me. I'll never forget that kindness.

Betty called my cousin Patsy Fleming to tell her to come get me. Patsy arrived with a car, helped me pack my bags, and drove me back to Mum's place in Toronto. Mum welcomed me with open arms and sat me down for a warm meal.

All kinds of interesting things happened in the following months. After having rested from housekeeping duties, I rejoined my friends from MRA. At one point, I found myself hurtling around Lac Saint-Jean in a yellow school-bus with my knees up to my chin. I was part of a group made up mostly of young people from Latin America and Quebec who were putting on a play called El Condor. I played the American ambassador's wife. We all spoke our own language on stage, a raucous mixture of Spanish, Portuguese, French and English. The loudspeaker was off and a French translation appeared over the stage.

We stayed in homes, convents, and in the nurses' residence of a large mental hospital. Then the cast took off westward, through the Rockies, down the coast and back through the unforgettable territory of the Navajo people. We played on black campuses in Georgia and at Florida State University. Everywhere we met students who were looking for a new direction for their lives and for the society we lived in. I roomed with a young Quebec actress. When we landed in Toronto, my mother served lunch to the whole cast and several of them stayed in our home.

Somewhere on that improbable trip, I decided to stop running away from life, and as best I could to run towards it, or through it or whatever. Nothing much changed that I noticed, but I was conscious of this new courage. I headed back to Canada get my bearings.

PERIBONKA

Back in Ontario, I spent a few weeks at Peribonka with my mother.

Front of Peribonka, ca. 1935, Catharine's mother's cottage, given by Granny Fleming as a wedding gift. Peribonka on Lake Simcoe, one hour north of Toronto, off the Tenth Concession, Innisville. Victoria worked with the architect to create an unusually spacious design.

As a wedding present, Granny Fleming had given my mum and dad the land and the money to build their own cottage next to hers. They chose the name Peribonka, after the river in Quebec where they had canoed during their honeymoon. At a time when most vacationers had small cabins, my mother surprised the architect with the spaciousness of her design, similar to the great cottages she had seen in the United States.

Living room of Peribonka with Catharine's father's photo on the table by the window and his sailing ship behind the sofa, ca. 1935

The living room was magnificent, with a huge stone fireplace. It was a storey-and-a-half high, with a large window looking out to the lake, glass doors on one side, and a balcony on the other side, above the long padded windowsill. The inside walls were lined with fragrant cedar.

Mum bought wicker chairs and a sofa from China. A picture of Dad stood in a place of honour on the long table, next to Grandmother's brass vase full of gladioli and the wooden model of a sailing vessel. An old wooden Victrola stood beside the fireplace, complete with a stack of vinyl records.

That room was the center of many gatherings. I remember rainy days when my cousins and I spent hours lying on the living room floor with the wood fire crackling, playing endless games of Monopoly. A game could last for as long as three days.

One summer Bill and Irene Clarke, founding editors of Clarke Irwin, one of Canada's foremost publishing houses, arrived at Peribonka with the manuscript of artist Emily Carr's soon to be famous memoir *Klee Wyck*. Sitting in front of the blazing living room fire, they took turns reading out loud. Mum and I were enthralled. Bill had only just managed to read; back in his college days, he had been declared legally blind. Irene had read the courses out loud and they both passed with honours.

Uncle Goldie built a cottage for his family next door to Peribonka and a diving tower out in the lake. Games of baseball, cricket and Prisoner's Base, along with swimming lessons from Mr. McCutcheon, kept us active. Then there was Playmate, the opinionated pony who usually tried to scrape me off his back with the help of the garage door. Only later, when I got caught up in a game of tag did I lose my fear of galloping at full speed.

My happiest memories of my mother are attached to Peribonka. Now that she was finally in charge of her own home, Mum was in her element, raking grass and pine cones while wearing comfortable slacks and a mosquito-proof jacket, or rocking for hours in her favourite wicker rocking chair on the spacious screened porch.

On Sundays, she allowed my cousins and me to be in charge of our own Sunday School. We could choose the hymns from the Methodist hymnbook and memorize a verse of our choice from the King James Version of the Bible. Imagine our irritation when my youngest cousin John Fleming found the shortest verse in that Bible for his choice. "And Jesus wept" went down in family history.

Our choice of hymns was not politically correct, but we belted out "Onward Christian Soldiers" with gusto. After Sunday School, Mum would throw all-day suckers on the lawn. Then we would have a swim, Sunday dinner and a nap.

Endless hours were spent in the tree house in the back field, built by Goldie's oldest son, Ross, and the twins, Bob and Lou. During the week, there were swims twice a day and trips out to the diving tower. I hated going into the water head first so I never got the hang of diving. I could only admire my cousin Barbara whose dive was so perfectly timed that her carefully pointed toes scarcely caused a ripple. I also remember Gary Clarke, son of publishers Bill and Irene Clarke, hitting his head on the diving board.

Next door to Uncle Goldie's own cottage was one that was rented summer after summer by the Kilbourns, mutual friends of the Clarkes and ours. Rosemary Kilbourn, a talented artist, remains a true friend to this day. Her brother Bill eventually became a dedicated mayor of Toronto.

The Kilbourns, the Clarkes and my mother were members of a unique Reading Club in Toronto. One winter they decided to study Beethoven. During the long winter evenings, the chords and themes of that master composer embedded themselves in my mind. Now when I hear those symphonies, I keep saying, "Thank you, Mum, what a gift you gave me." And as a teenager, I loved dressing up when she took me to the occasional symphony.

Music had been an integral part of my mother's early years at the family home on St. Clair Avenue. At Lake Simcoe, Uncle Goldie carried on the family tradition of singing the old Methodist hymns around the piano on Sunday night. Cousins Ross and Barbara could play by ear.

On hot August nights at Peribonka, Mum and I would sometimes stay up later than usual and go down to sit on the beach in deck chairs. Looking up at the starry sky, I would feel a growing sense of wonder. There were all those myriad tiny lights flickering in the darkness.

There were Cassiopeia and Orion. I could see the three stars that formed Orion's belt. There were other constellations whose names I didn't know, but whose formation was sometimes clear. I would sense my own spirit expanding in response to the magnitude of it all. Just the simple wonder of being. I didn't have to do anything or achieve anything.

PACE MAGAZINE

One day in 1965 the phone rang. This call would prove to be a major turning point in my life, with its invitation by my cousin Robert Fleming to join the staff of *Pace* magazine in Los Angeles as Research Editor. I headed out on the next plane, then by bus, to the imposing building at 833 South Flower Street in downtown Los Angeles.

Bob had co-founded *Pace* with Stu Lancaster as a large-format international picture magazine designed to inspire world youth, ages 19-34. Bob's photographs for the magazine were outstanding. He took photographs in forty-seven countries over his lifetime. John Hallward came on board as publisher. Soon after, Al Kuettner, former editor of the *Atlanta Herald*, joined the team. A group of highly talented people was coming together.

My job was to come up with fifty to one hundred
story ideas each month for the editors and writers. What
an incredible excuse to get out and meet a vast range of
personalities, or talk to them on the phone.

Each month I scoured newspapers and talked to people
all over the country, looking for cutting edge ideas and people
who had something to say. This included White House Fellows,
longshoreman Eric Hoffer, Canadian underwater explorer
Joe MacInnis, and the editor of the *Michigan Law Review*. At
the navy's Sealab, a chap in a wetsuit told me solemnly, "Man
is going back under the sea." I had a reason to talk to young
people on farms, and to find out what possessed a 16-year-old
Olympic swimmer to spend so many hours in a wet bathing
suit. I tracked down Nancy Greene and her whole Canadian
ski team up a mountain in British Columbia, to the excitement
of the Los Angeles telephone operator.

I stayed with a family who lent me their pink Jaguar
while they were away. For weeks I clocked up hundreds of
miles, going out to meet the most interesting people I could
find. I wanted to reflect the texture of real life back into the
magazine and break out of the cocoon of old ideas and ways
of thinking. The editors were occasionally exasperated when
I was not to be found, but many of the ideas I placed on their
desks each month turned into articles.

One day I drove out into the desert to meet the two
beer-bellied builders of the longest car in the world. I was
curious to know what motivated two gas station owners to
go beyond the ordinary. "It's like climbing a mountain," one of
them said. "It's just there in you."

One morning, a paragraph in the *Los Angeles Times*
caught my eye. It was the story of a sixteen-year-old boy,
Robin Lee Graham. He had just set out from Watchorn Basin,
intending to sail solo around the world in a 24-foot Lapworth

sloop named Dove. He brought with him two kittens named Suzette and Joliette.

I borrowed a car, drove down to the harbour, and was able to track down Robin's aunt. She said to me, "Robin and his family never think, 'This is going to be dangerous so I won't do it.'" She put me in touch with his parents who owned an avocado farm down the coast. They told me how to get in touch with Robin by sending letters ahead to Honolulu and Fiji.

One day, there to my delight was a letter from Robin.

> My toughest moment was when I broke my mast. It was October 19, 1965. I'd been fifteen days out from Fanning Island when I sighted Tutuila (American Samoa). I was very happy about that.
>
> I was sailing along pretty good when I hit a squall and within less than a heartbeat the mast was overboard. That's when the work really started. It wasn't easy.

In fact, Robin himself had been swept overboard as he tried to pull the sails and rigging back into the boat. Somehow he managed. He was able to make it to Samoa. In a later letter, he described falling sleep, then waking suddenly to see a huge freighter bearing down on him.

In another letter he wrote, "This is more fun than sitting in front of a T.V. set or going to wild parties." Still, at times he experienced profound loneliness and even despair. That changed on the Fiji Islands when he met a beautiful girl from California, Patti Ratteree.

Patti was hitchhiking, working and sometimes riding a motorcycle around the world. They fell in love and spent idyllic weeks diving for shells among the coral reefs, fishing and living off the land. The understanding was that Robin had to continue his journey alone. Sadly they parted, not sure if they would ever meet again.

They met again in South Africa, after Dove had been reported lost at sea. By a miracle, Robin had managed to keep the boat steady in thirty-foot waves. He finished the trip but by this time he had had enough of solitary adventure. He and Patti got married, had a baby, and headed for a new life in Montana, where Robin got work in construction. *National Geographic* did a major two-issue story on their journey. It received more reader response than any in its history. Back in Los Angeles, I wrote up the story. The harbour newspaper lent me photos and I presented my first scoop to *Pace*.

Unfortunately, Robin was no longer on speaking terms with the father who had encouraged this trip. His dad had been afraid that the connection with Patti would interfere with his son's goals. I phoned Robin's parents from Los Angeles when I was on my way to start work at *Pace's* New York office. Robin's dad sounded heartbroken.

"Catharine, there's a book there that will never be written." With only ten minutes before my plane left Los Angeles airport, I had time to make just one phone call. I phoned South African writer Derek Gill, senior editor at *Pace* in Los Angeles.

"Derek, do something," I said and gave him Robin's phone number.

Derek arranged for Robin, Patti and the baby to move into the house next door. They worked effectively together. The result was the book *Dove*. It was translated into fourteen languages and caught the imagination of young people around the world.

From that one phone call I learned the power each of us has to make creative connections. From Robin Graham I caught the excitement of following our own deepest dreams in spite of the risks. And when we do, the universe brings all sorts of energy to help us.

The book was made into the movie *The Dove* in 1974, produced by Gregory Peck. I had the privilege of sitting in the audience for the New York premiere. It was chosen in England for a Royal Command performance. Close to a million people flocked to the film in China alone.

Catharine's scoop for *Pace* magazine led to this book and a movie that was shown around the world.

On my seventy-fifth birthday, in 2005, I received the most heartwarming letter from Robin.

> I hope you have a wonderful party to-day. You have played an important part in our lives. Many years ago you wrote an article in *Pace* magazine about my leaving in a small boat to sail around the world. When I returned home you encouraged Derek Gill to get in touch with us and help write our adventures in a book. Dove was not only a blessing to Derek and us but to many, many other people. After 35 years we are still receiving letters and meeting some wonderful people because of it.
>
> Thank you for your involvement in our lives.
>
> Robin and Patti Graham

A single phone call had an impact. Just as the ripple of a butterfly's wing is said to set in motion a wave that has an effect on the other side of the world, something we say or do, some dream we have, can be of greater significance than we realize.

During my time in Los Angeles, life at *Pace* was a stimulating adventure. One whole issue was devoted to the new Russia, an innovative approach after the McCarthy era that had affected so many academics and Hollywood people.

California was full of unusual people such as the actor Steve McQueen who rode motorcycles full tilt in the desert, and the surfer who went looking for the perfect wave. I tracked down this surfer at his ranch up the Coast, and this turned into one of *Pace's* most memorable photo essays.

Pace itself was a phenomenon. In the middle of the ferment of the Sixties, it offered young people alternatives to the high of drugs: the stimulation of living life to the fullest. The founding editors, Bob Fleming and Stu Lancaster, brought a level of imagination and intelligence to their work that earned them the respect of the forty strong personalities who worked at the magazine and their readers. The readers included people in government and the professions as well as an ever-increasing number of young people. The magazine was nearly bought out by Hearst Corporation before it finally folded at the end of the Sixties, along with other large format magazines.

During my time in California, I reconnected with Denise Hyde who had been the translator for Irène Laure at Caux. She had married John Wood and they moved to Pasadena, California. At that time, the city of Pasadena was polarized between black, white and Hispanic citizens. Denise was asked by their Anglican Church to "listen to the city" for a year and feed back what she heard to some of the businessmen. She called the process "Creative Connections." She reached out to people from all the different sectors of the city's life and invited each of them to a brown-bag lunch at a table outside the church. She found that if people could get off their turf, outside the limitations of their own mandate, it made all the difference.

When Denise asked a young lad why he had joined a gang, he told her, "They threatened to shoot my dog in front of me if I didn't." She visited the mayor. He asked her to reach out to a black agitator who had been demonstrating outside his office. She went to visit that man on his farm and discovered that he was writing an opera. They talked at length. Much later he teased her with, "How come an old white woman like you put me back in touch with my black kids?"

Out of Denise's conversations with Pasadena's citizens that year, a consensus emerged. Seven new initiatives for young people, with some state funding, were put in place. The Creative Connections process continues to this day. In August

of 1995, at the wedding reception for Anne Hallward, daughter
of our friends John and Clare, I heard Denise retelling some
of the stories. I invited her to come to the meditation centre
on Pine Avenue to meet with Montrealers from different
backgrounds. The ripple effect of that gathering continues to
this day. An architect, who used to work in the inner city but
had lost hope, met the founder of the second largest food bank
in Montreal. He got himself on her board, helped her start a
newspaper, then initiated get-togethers with other groups. A
neighbour of ours got herself on the board of a mental health
organization where she brought fresh insights and energy.

Pace opened up an office in New York and I spent a year
there. The widow of an Anglican bishop lent me the most
beautiful apartment I had ever seen just near the East River.
It was the first time in years I had had a base that was both
quiet and stable. Every evening I went out to wait for the first
section of the *New York Times* at the local street vendor. I read
it while munching a slice of cheese and tomato pizza. I went
back three times to see Pearl Bailey in *Hello, Dolly*. The whole
city was energizing.

That summer we moved the *Pace* office onto an old
army base on an island an hour north of New York. Suddenly
hundreds of young people began arriving on the island from
all over the United States. The first *Up With People* show was
put together with the help of the three Colwell brothers who
had gotten their start in Hollywood. They had introduced
themselves to us at the *Pace* building on South Flower Street
in Los Angeles. Herbie Allan, cofounder of *Up With People*,
played the xylophone with exuberance.

I had difficulty walking because of the hip dysplasia
I had been born with. Luckily, on the island, I could bicycle
everywhere, to the outdoor cookouts and to the army hut
where *Pace* had set up camp. It was a wonderful summer. I felt

part of an explosion of energy working itself out through *Pace* and *Up With People*.

As I bicycled, I realized it was time for a change. I was 38. It was clear that *Pace* would not continue forever. Back home, my mother needed my help while she sold the farm near Aurora, Ontario that she had bought as a gathering place for the family. I spent the next two years on that farm, forty minutes north of Toronto.

Toronto 1968 – 1972

Writing Speeches at Queen's Park

Once more, I was back in the rolling Ontario farmland I thought I had said good-bye to forever. There were no animals, but the white stucco house was full of sunlight and color. I hadn't realized how bone-tired I was. For almost two years I hibernated on an unexpected sabbatical. The old tension between my mother and me had evaporated. We were glad to be together after the long years of separation.

When the farm was sold, I applied for a job in intergovernmental affairs with the Ontario government, indicating a special interest in Quebec. While I waited, I took every French course I could find. Down at Queen's Park, I saw an ad for a three-week subsidized trip to Japan to see the Ontario pavilion at Osaka's Expo. There were still a few seats available, so I applied and was accepted. When I told Bob Fleming that I was going to Japan, he gave me one last assignment for *Pace*, to find out what Japan's interest in Canada would be. This took me into conversations with the editors of Japan's two largest newspapers. I was received with a formal tea ceremony.

Back in Toronto, an article about the connections I had made in Japan appeared on the editorial page of Toronto's *Financial Post*. It brought a phone call from the Ministry of Multiculturalism and Community Development. Would I come in for an interview? The next morning I was ushered into a room with two men. The taller of the two, the Deputy Minister, peered down at me from a height of 6'4". He said, "Catharine, would you be interested in writing some speeches?" The other, an outgoing, jolly looking man added, "I am invited to make speeches all over the province. Often it is only the chance to say thank you to the hundreds of people working away in their small groups. I want to give them a chance to be heard, and answer their questions. I want speeches that carry some meaning." This was the Minister of Multiculturalism and Community Development, my future boss Robert Welch.

I rocked back on my heels. I thought to myself, "If these two are crazy enough to think I can do it, who am I to say I can't?" I had scribbled since childhood but I had never written a speech in my life. At *Pace* I had found writing even a short piece extremely hard work.

I reported in to my immediate superior a week later. He was a bright 24-year-old sociology graduate from the University of Toronto. I was 40. When he discovered I had never written a speech in my life he was furious. "They've sent me a researcher," he fumed. The Minister was a fine orator who kept his staff stretched to the limit to keep up with his speaking schedule. The Ministry was into empowering women, so my sociologist superior put his mind to mentoring me into writing good speeches even if it killed me. It nearly did. "You *must* have something to say," he bellowed in despair as he read my wooden drafts of an address to the African Violet Society or the Ukrainian refugees.

In September, the sociologist left for an indefinite stay in Europe, no doubt much needed. A hotshot writer from *Maclean's* was hired to replace him. I was gently told I would be moved to another part of the Ministry. No speeches. I persuaded the Minister to let me stay in the department a little longer, with an assignment to write one speech a week. The hotshot left in a huff four days later, in protest at the workload. The Deputy Minister came roaring into my office saying, "Catharine, we have an emergency. The Minister is to give a major speech on Canada in Los Angeles."

I asked a junior secretary what she thought a Canadian was. "I think Canadians are communicators of a new society," she said without thinking. I thought, "Eureka! I've got it." I found a joke to start off the speech, then wove a few paragraphs around the theme. Later, the young secretary could not remember having said or thought such a thing. The speech was a huge success. The Minister knew how to lift what I wrote off the page and turn it into a spellbinder. I was rehired.

The next speech was the Estimates. It was a major test for the whole Department, the one chance to get a decent amount of money voted by the Legislature. My final draft was a disaster. I had included ideas from one of the department heads whom the Deputy disapproved of. He was grim as he left our meeting. At three o'clock in the morning, I got up and reworked the whole speech. It was accepted. The entire team on my floor pitched in to get the speech typed and copied in time to distribute to all members of the Legislature.

The speech was well received. The Minister was then shifted to a new cabinet post as Minister of Education, while I stayed where I was. To my amusement, department heads began coming to me asking for help with their speeches. I had my own wood-panelled office in a homey, three storey office building just off Bloor Street. That area was a convergence for people from all of the different countries who had come to Toronto after the war. You could hear seventy languages spoken if you stood long enough on one corner. I used to sit over a cup of coffee in the Hungarian restaurant to work on speeches, away from the phone, content with the low buzz of conversation going on around me.

Although I still hoped to get there, Quebec was no place to go to at that time. Headlines proclaimed the latest Fédération de la Libération du Québec mailbox bombing. A colleague rushed in to tell us the War Measures Act had been declared. Tanks were rolling towards Montreal. I walked into the street, stunned by the realization that in Canada, our civil liberties could be suspended. It had happened to friends in Europe; I didn't expect that it could happen to me. The sight of the Italian vendor across the street dishing out popcorn, and an Indian woman dressed in a beautiful sari, carrying her baby, were immensely reassuring. Later, a friend in Belfast told me, "We discovered that our greatest weapon against terrorism was to maintain the normalcy of our everyday lives." That sunny morning I experienced this for myself.

The people working with me in the Bloor Street building were a cohesive and hardworking group. I enjoyed writing some of their fresh ideas into the Minister's speeches. I liked to think I was nudging the procedures and policy of government just a little. When I needed to discuss the next Estimates speech with the new Minister of Citizenship, I walked into his office as usual. One of his staff was appalled. "Who is this woman?" The new head of our Communications team, Frank Moritsugu, shrugged. "She is a free spirit." Frank was a tough ex-newspaperman with a sense of humour. He let me be.

Three months later, I was hired back on Bob Welch's staff in the Ministry of Education, now housed on the twenty-second floor of the brand new Mowat Block, a stone's throw from the massive red brick pile that houses the Ontario Legislature. My father had courted my mother at one of the red brick houses just down the street after Grandmother had moved the whole family into the city for the winter in 1929.

I was amused to note that a certain status attached itself to offices on the twenty-second floor, with easy access to the Minister. My sociologist boss was back from Europe to write speeches. He found me a cubbyhole with a desk. It was noisy but fun, with the mandarins of the Ministry constantly arriving for meetings. I got to know many of the officers at all levels of government. One colleague, in particular, helped me to find my way around the labyrinth. Joy Gordon was a talented writer who had written many speeches for Bill Davis, later the Premier of Ontario. Soon she would move over to his staff. We worked together on speeches, often until ten o'clock at night. I spent a wonderful holiday at her home in Jamaica.

There was a good deal of infighting in the Ministry of Education, between the mandarins and teachers on the front line in the classroom. I had finagled a larger office space. Now I started to throw doughnut parties to bring some of these people together. I had fun editing out of the Minister's speeches some of the more restrictive attitudes that departmental die-hards tried to foist on us.

An ambitious report by an outside consulting firm threw the department into total chaos. Desks were going up in the elevator and a few minutes later coming back down. No one knew where they were supposed to be working or with whom. Some of the most creative people were getting ready to quit. Senior officials did nothing. Another woman and I went to see the Minister. At our suggestion, a series of meetings were held to sort things out. This was not on my job description, but as a friend from the days of Caux said, "We learned to look around at the whole community, see what needed to be done, and do something about it."

MEETING NEIL ON THE DANCE FLOOR

About this time, I saw an ad in the Toronto *Globe and Mail* for "Hiatus, an arts and letters society with a sense of humour." It sounded like just the ticket, a good balance to my six-day work week. Members invited interesting guests to their homes, or went to the theatre, concerts and dances. There were no dues. Volunteers sent out a mimeographed list of events. The first evening I attended was at a member's home to hear the historian, Ramsay Cook, an expert on Quebec's Quiet Revolution. The host was a friend of his, a tall, quiet, rather distant chap. I didn't pay much attention to him. I learned only his name, Neil McKenty, and that he was a former Jesuit.

I went to several theatre events. I decided that on the whole the women members of Hiatus were more interesting than the men. By this time, I had shaken my fist at heaven, demanding to know where was this husband my aunts and my mother had been dutifully praying for since the years at Donlands. I wasn't all that impressed with this prayer stuff. Having gotten that off my chest, I made up my mind to live my life to the hilt. If it happened to coincide with someone else's that was fine. If it didn't, fine.

One evening I dropped in to a Hiatus dance. I was standing chatting to some friends when my host of the Quebec evening appeared at my elbow and asked me to dance. He was 6'1", just the right height for my 5'8-1/2". He danced with an innate sense of rhythm and a simple step I could easily follow. We chatted away on the dance floor. Suddenly, an unexpected thought came roaring through my mind. It had a bell-like clarity. "This is the man I am going to marry." I was so startled, I almost missed a step. He was unlike anything I had pictured in my girlhood dreams.

At college I had worn a fraternity pin. There had been several romances along the way. This man was utterly different.

On our first date, I discovered this man was anything but silent. I concluded he was opinionated, autocratic, utterly impossible, and immensely interesting. He escorted me home in a taxi, then exerted pressure to come in with me as though it were his divine right. I sent him packing and thought that's that. For the next six months I concentrated on my work, with a running commentary playing in the back of my mind, sorting out the little I knew about this exasperating personage. I kept returning to that moment of complete clarity and certainty. I moved to another apartment and dated other people.

One evening, I picked up the *Toronto Star*. There was Neil McKenty's name in a rave article by Scott Fisher about his biography of Mitch Hepburn, published a few years earlier in 1967. I picked up the phone and asked Neil if he had seen the article. Of course he had, but he now had my new phone number. A week later, I dropped in on a Hiatus party. There was one seat left at a table opposite McKenty. I sat down with a feeling of coming home. Neither of us spoke a word to the other throughout the whole meal.

We both fetched our coats and as we were leaving, one of the men in the Club rushed up and said, "Oh Catharine, can I have your phone number? I want to ask you out." That did it. Neil was put on his mettle. He escorted me home in a taxi, no pressure to come in this time, and for the next nine nights and one day, he invited me out for a date.

The next ten days were a whirlwind. We went out every evening to places that were free and interesting, including a nude bar, usually stopping to pick up the 9:00 p.m. edition of the *Globe and Mail*. On Saturday, we spent the whole day almost completely in silence, taking a picnic to Centre Island where we sat on the grass. Neil read the newspapers while I watched the Canada geese, absorbing the whole remarkable turn of events. "This will work," Neil said at the end of the day. I didn't need convincing.

During those ten days, Neil and I were very candid with each other about our checkered careers. He even told me about a time in England when he went to explore the red light district near the Thames. A drunken sailor coming off a boat punched him in the eye and broke his glasses, injuring one eye. He ended up in hospital. The newspapers made the most of a headline about a Jesuit injured in the red light district. "I was just curious," he said, "but my superiors were not amused."

In fact, Neil was so brutally honest about himself that I wondered if it weren't time he took a much longer look at his good qualities. I remember thinking, "This is a very special human being." There were no hidden secrets, including the fact that he was a recovering alcoholic. He told me that when he crashed his car into the front porch of his Superior's residence, the Jesuits had sent him to Southdown, a rehab centre near Aurora, north of Toronto, where he spent six months. He went to A.A., stopped drinking and got the traction to leave the Jesuits. Then for three years he greatly enjoyed working with Red Foster, the Kennedys, and Brian O'Neill of the National Hockey League to bring the Special Olympics with floor hockey to Canada. Pierre Elliott Trudeau dropped the first puck at Maple Leaf Gardens.

Magnificent yellow roses and telegrams started arriving at my Queen's Park office. My colleagues were intrigued. On the tenth day, Sunday, I dropped by Neil's place at 4 Oaklands Avenue on my way to a family birthday party. With all his Jesuit skill, Neil posed a question I couldn't say no to. "You know I want to marry you, don't you?" he asked. I said, "Well, yes." It was hardly romantic, but as far as I was concerned, that settled it. I went joyously off to Aunt Stella's party. That evening, knowing Aunt Stella was rabidly anti-Catholic and that my mother would disapprove as none of my boyfriends ever measured up to my dad, I told the news to my cousins. They all ganged up on my mother and Aunt Stella with congratulations, who were both left speechless. As a way of avoiding a family Donnybrook, I thought it was a master coup. Years later, my mother would describe this scene with relish.

The next week, however, my mother summoned Neil to a high level meeting to explain why we shouldn't get married. She was sure I was getting married out of desperation at age forty-one. She started off by saying, "You know, Neil, that Catharine has a malformed hip that causes her quite a bit of pain." "Victoria," he said in his most regal tones, "we'll get an operation." She tried a couple of other arguments, then, with Dad always in her head, said, "You know, Neil, Catharine's family has been praying all her life that she would find the right husband." All Neil's training went into his answer. "Victoria," he said, "your prayers have been answered!" Mum knew she'd met her match. She started to laugh, and they began to plan the wedding.

MARRIAGE

The shockwaves of my decision rippled along the telephone wires. Aunt Stella made copies of my father's speeches, warning about the dangers of being taken over by Rome; a low blow, I thought. My dad had grown up in Peterborough in the heart of Orange country; his father, a local merchant, had founded a Baptist church. Aunt Ev warned of too hasty a step. She had broken off her own engagement after a fight with her fiancé at the airport. In true Fleming style she had never changed her mind.

Was I crazy? What did I really know about this man? The answer was that I simply knew he was the one for me. The rest would have to take care of itself. He had told me about his earlier pattern of heavy drinking, so I was aware of the risks. I was also aware of the respect and affection I had for my Uncle Lloyd, also a recovering alcoholic. It was a move toward life and love.

In the six weeks before the ceremony, my family pitched in to get invitations printed and to complete all the arrangements. I found a dress hanging on the rack at Simpson's that matched the long Brussels lace train my mother had hidden away years before without my knowing. My cousin Lydia organized the bridesmaids' dresses, while her parents, along with my cousin Barbara, pitched in with other details. I was slightly in a daze with the speed of all this. Sensing that, Neil insisted I come and sit beside him in a lawn chair in the garden of his home for an afternoon of silence.

We were married in August of 1972. Canon Dann of the Anglican Cathedral came back from holidays ready to perform the marriage ceremony. Neil's friend, Fr. Edward Dowling, was there to assist Canon Dann at the service. I had from Canon Dann a note agreeing to officiate, in which he added the comment, "Your fiancé will have heard the story about the Jewish lad going with the Catholic girl. She wouldn't marry him unless he took instruction from the priest, which he did. One evening he had to break the sad news that the wedding was off, saying, 'I've been oversold. I'm to be a priest!'" I was amused.

Mum had asked that we be married in my High Anglican school chapel so that she wouldn't have to explain things to her friends at Timothy Eaton Memorial Church.

Archbishop Pocock gave permission for Neil to be married in a Protestant ceremony, respecting the fact that my father was a Protestant minister. My mother saw the Anglican ceremony as a compromise between our two family traditions.

Catharine and Neil's wedding in Toronto in 1972

Eventually my mother came to feel that she and Neil had a great deal in common. A mutual affection developed that pleased me enormously. She said to me on the phone, "I think there is a special contribution you and Neil are going to make together."

I can't say enough about the way the Jesuits accepted me. I was treated as one of the family. At one point, Neil and I were invited to a quiet private mass at the Jesuit Residence. I was offered the Eucharist as a matter of course. None of this "only Catholics in good standing are allowed" which always seemed to me the opposite of the inclusiveness of Jesus.

At the Hunt Club reception laid on by my Uncle Murray, Neil blithely dispensed with the formalities of a reception line. Instead, we mingled with our friends on the lawn by the lake in the August sunshine, sipping cool drinks. My mother had insisted there be no alcohol served at the dinner itself, in keeping with her own firm beliefs. As we went up the stairs to enter the clubhouse dining room, a waiter stood at the entrance with a tray, ready to take away our glass of wine or spirits. Neil quietly picked up my full glass of wine from the tray, carried it with him and plunked it firmly down at my place.

After the meal and the toasts to the bride, Neil got up to speak. As my mother listened, she visibly relaxed, leaning back in her chair with a contented, "Ah." She told me later that publisher Irene Clarke had said to her, "I always wondered where Catharine would find the brains," a compliment that pleased me immensely, coming from her.

Mother was quite relieved that most of her huge circle of friends were out of the city and could not attend. She was still taken aback that I had married a Catholic. She left immediately after the wedding to recoup at the home of my cousins Lou and Val in London, England. Neil moved out of

the house Red Foster had lent him and into my apartment at
130 Russell Hill Road.

The day after we returned from our honeymoon we
started packing. Neil had applied for and won, out of 60
applicants, the job as Public Affairs Director at CJAD Radio
in Montreal. We were headed down the 401. I realized how
easily we might have missed each other if I had not seen the
ad in the *Globe and Mail* or phoned him after our disastrous
first date.

MONTREAL 1972 – 1982

DIFFICULT EARLY DAYS

It was clear from the first day of our arrival in Montreal that I was dealing with an autocrat who was used to having his own way. We looked at several apartments. I preferred a spacious two-bedroom with a view of the mountain. No indeed. We took a cheaper single-bedroom on the twenty-first floor of a narrow building right behind the NHL hockey rink, the Forum. His microphone took over my linen closet. Occasionally, the power went out. If we had lunch guests, Neil would walk down the stairs and bring the guests trudging up twenty-one floors. When I enquired about the name of the owner, I was told in no uncertain terms, "Don't ask." We were, however, given an empty apartment for our wedding gifts and extra belongings. The door would be unlocked for me by a young man with a gun on his hip.

I could look out the window and watch a famous cop, Lukashek, walking along the sidewalk, covered by his wife, walking three feet behind him with a gun in her hand.

Fortunately, there was a convenience store right across the street where I could buy basic groceries, since I was walking with more and more pain in my hip.

The Greek restaurants on Prince Arthur were a steady attraction for us on weekends. Who could resist a shish kebab cooked to perfection at a reasonable price, with the chance to sit indoors or outdoors, depending on the season.

We took the number 24 bus along Sherbrooke Street as far as St. Denis Street, then transferred to the bus going north for the short distance to St. Louis Square. The first time we did this, we walked across the park full of families with children, couples and the occasional itinerant. As we neared the entrance to Prince Arthur Street, the strains of a Beethoven melody wafted towards us. A trio of young musicians were playing their hearts out, and continued to do so for the rest of the evening. I saw this as an auspicious beginning for us.

Often, we went exploring all over the city on the bus, seeing how far we could get on one bus ticket each. Some of our anglophone friends told us they had never gone further east than Boulevard St. Laurent, the midpoint of the city. We traversed this cultural line into the French neighbourhoods, to the most eastern point of Montreal, Pointe-aux-Trembles, or had lunch out east at the colourful Botanical Gardens along with the Italian wedding couples. That first winter I remember waiting for the bus on Sherbrooke Street. The icy wind blowing snow down that wind tunnel was so penetrating that I was almost sobbing with cold. I learned how to dress in layers; I bought a warmer coat and a big Montreal woollen tuque. Once, in the middle of a snowstorm, we discovered Schwartz's Diner with its smoked meat sandwiches sitting on the counter, warm sawdust on the floor and blazing grill. We went back often on weekends.

On one freezing winter day, standing at a bus stop by the Olympic Stadium in a blowing snowstorm, we decided that we had to "join the winter or perish." We bought two cheap pairs of cross-country skis and went skiing in the

Montreal parks. We found a lovely winding trail on Mount Royal. Mac McCurdy was manager at CJAD at the time. He and his wife invited us to ski near their home, then told us about the Laurentian Lodge Ski Club. Neil has mentioned in his memoir the role that the Club would play in our lives. We later wrote a book about the Club, the adventure of skiing in the Laurentians, and a history of the Laurentian Mountains themselves.

The first weekend we went to the club, I arrived wearing my usual outfit of jacket and ski pants. After a long day of skiing in which I felt such a part of the club, we went in for supper. I walked into the dining room wearing my ski clothes. The other women took one look at me and escorted me upstairs, where I was lent a silk blouse and long woolen skirt. Neil was lent a tie and jacket. We laughed a lot at the table about this, and then and there the members decided we would do.

A bright spot in that first year of marriage was the friendship with Sister Gertrude McLaughlin, whom we met through a friend. She was an honorary Methodist, so she understood where I was coming from as a Methodist married to a Catholic. Sr. Gertrude made a huge difference to these early years in Montreal. She guided us on trips to the east end of the city, and later when we had a car, out to the countryside, exploring the back country lanes, the small country villages and historic sites.

Another highlight of that first winter was being invited to the Canadiens hockey games at the Forum by Brian O'Neill. Neil had worked with him to bring the Special Olympics to Canada. We sat right behind the goal. Brian and Jean O'Neill were hospitality itself that first winter, inviting us to their home for Christmas and other occasions. Despite such kindness, the stress of being crammed into a small space with a man I hardly knew was beginning to take its toll, along with the pain in my hip, a long winter and a strange city.

However, that first Christmas, Neil gave me a small parcel that enchanted me. It contained a small disc with a recording of two songs. The first one was the hit from My Fair Lady, "I Could Have Danced All Night." The second was, "May I Have This Dance for the Rest of My Life?"

He said quietly, "Those songs express better than any words of mine what was going through my head that first night you and I met."

Fr. Ed, who was Assistant to the Jesuit Provincial, came to visit us at our home in Montreal, bringing with him Neil's medical records. Reading them frankly scared the hell out of me. What had I gotten myself into?

I knew Neil had spent six months at Southdown, the Roman Catholic rehabilitation centre north of Toronto. That had given him the traction to leave the Jesuits and start a new life. I had no idea, however, that Neil had been locked up in a Jesuit mental hospital after a bout of suicidal depression. The word "bipolar" was not mentioned in that transcript, nor in anything that Neil ever wrote. Harold Thuringer, Neil's close friend, told me that Neil had discussed the implications of his condition without mentioning the term. Neil himself told me that the psychologist at the Jesuit lockup centre didn't like him much and said to him, "If you'd just get off your ass and get going, you'd be alright," without prescribing any medication.

Neil's doctor told us that if he had known Neil was bipolar at the beginning, it would have helped him in this choice of treatment. It was also much later that I began to read about this condition and its implications. I found Jessie Close's honest autobiography very helpful. Jesse was the younger sister of the actress Glenn Close, and although her father was a doctor, her condition was not identified for many years.

Even though there was a small grocery store, or *dépanneur* as we called it in Montreal, right across the street from our apartment, my left hip was causing me more and more pain as I lugged bags home and tried to clean the house. We were crammed into an apartment smaller than the space either of us had been accustomed to for ourselves, living on Neil's half-salary without a car. I was still looking for a job as a researcher or even as a writer. We were far from our families and friends, in unfamiliar surroundings, and I was not used to living in close quarters with someone so verbally fast on the draw.

One day, we were having a lively lunch with some of Neil's CJAD colleagues. I chipped in with a comment about the topic at hand and he interrupted me sharply with, "What are you saying that for?" I was startled and hurt. This added to my growing sense that something was seriously out of kilter with this marriage. It was clear that this man was used to getting his own way, and had very little idea of the give and take of relationships.

Our first Christmas I was so angry I swept all the dishes off our tiny table with a sweep of the arm. Coke went flying all over our cream-coloured sofa. Neil got quietly up and headed for the door. I thought, "He's gone. I'll never see him again. This is the end." A few minutes later, Neil walked calmly in and took me out to a nice dinner at the Alpenhaus. He had sensibly gone around the block for a walk. As I scrubbed the coke off the sofa, I thought, "I'll never have to do that again." He had discovered that he could push me only so far.

However, I began to wonder whether we shouldn't end the marriage before too much time went by. One day I snapped at him that if he hadn't been in the Jesuits for twenty-six years, he'd have been a high-priced lawyer with three divorces behind him. We didn't speak for twenty-four hours, then he carried on as though nothing had happened.

On one occasion, I was in Toronto just about to go out for a lovely supper at the Rosedale Golf Club with my cousin Everett Fleming and his wife Freddy. Before going into the restaurant, I phoned Neil and got an earful about something that had triggered his anger. My mood changed to depression, as though a light had gone out. I faked happiness throughout supper. That incident taught me to pace myself with phone calls and conversations, especially on important occasions.

It was only later that I read about the rise in stress levels that any change can make. I didn't know what had hit me physically, mentally and emotionally.

COUNSELLING

After only a few short months, I said to Neil I thought we should seriously consider calling it quits. After all, we hadn't been married that long. He said nothing that evening, except, "Do you honestly think there will be no damage?" Two days later he told me he'd set up an appointment with a marriage counsellor named Tobi Klein. He came with me to the first appointment, then left me to it alone.

That didn't bother Tobi at all. "I don't do counselling the way other people do," she told me. "I'll show you how to deal with him." I discovered only later that she had apparently said to Neil, "Don't worry, she worships the ground you walk on." When she heard about the groceries and the pain in the hip that had been malformed at birth, she sent me to the Jewish General where a first-rate Indian doctor in the physiotherapy department arranged an intensive treatment plan that soon began to take effect. Her exercises strengthened the muscles around the hip to such an extent that I was able to chug along behind Neil, straight up the far side of Mount Royal on a lovely summer day.

Tobi was a good and gentle listener. One day she surprised me by saying, "Your clothes are terrible." She gave me the name of a talented dress designer from Persia, Farah Youssefi, who created some unique and inexpensive outfits from lovely materials, some of which I have kept for over 40 years.

During all the years I had been an MRA volunteer with no salary, my mother had paid for my clothes, but it had never occurred to her to let me choose my own wardrobe. She had taken me to the best stores and had always overseen the purchases. With a closet full of her choices, I dressed richly but very conservatively. Now Farah Youssefi was creating for me a much more youthful look and I was having twice the fun doing my own thing.

Looking back, I realize that the pressure of marrying a man I hardly knew, moving to Montreal where I knew almost no one and being without a job triggered a return of the old pattern of anxiety and depression. With Tobi's help, that began lifting and I was able to laugh again. I could see my life from a lighter perspective.

Eventually, Neil was given a second-hand Chevrolet as part of his salary package. When he got behind the wheel of that car, Neil's mood was always cheerier. We both loved exploring the city and had our best conversations while we were driving. Neil once asked me, "How come we talk so easily in the car?" We went for long drives out to the edges of Montreal, sometimes stopping on the way for coffee or for lunch at our favourite restaurants. On other days, it would be over Montreal's urban mountain, Mount Royal, or further away to Pointe-Claire. A favorite destination was the West Island, where we could explore new restaurants for lunch.

One couple told us how amused they were watching us sit in total silence throughout the whole meal except when the waiter came.

Sometimes, however, Neil would turn on American conservative talk radio in the car, to my annoyance. He liked to hear what the opposition was saying. I drew the line at the obnoxious Rush Limbaugh, though. If he came on, I would switch the dial to another station regardless of Neil's protests.

During those drives, we always stopped at a restaurant for coffee and a sour cream doughnut. I would grab a table while Neil went to the counter to place our order. Sometimes I would ask for icing but, mindful of sugar, I would more often join Neil in asking for just plain. Often Neil would bring along our morning *Gazette* which he would share with me, a companionable moment in the day. Neil usually read at least three newspapers a day, the *New York Times*, the *Globe and Mail*, and of course the *Montreal Gazette*. Each week he would also read *The Monitor*, *Westmount Examiner*, and *The Senior Times*. When he had time to spend at the library, he would dip into the British newspapers. The news and opinions in these papers were meat and drink to Neil. I was always amazed at how quickly he absorbed their contents and how much that work enriched his comments on radio and in conversation.

On longer trips to Kingston and Toronto, Neil had an uncanny knack for discovering the location of every Tim Hortons doughnut shop on or near Highway 401. A great way to break the journey. This knack amazed me because Neil was "directionally challenged," as they say, with a talent for getting lost, even on streets in Montreal which he had travelled again and again. He simply refused to read maps.

Often, all I could do was go back to the blinding certainty I had had that very first time I danced with Neil, "This is the man I'm going to marry," with the conviction that the thought was from God. Now I had an image of Neil's guardian angel and mine saying to each other, "Let's put these two together and see what happens."

I thought about my Dad starting a school and an orphanage in India with his brothers. I thought about my mother and her courage as she set out on her life after Dad's death while she was four months pregnant with me. And my widowed Granny, who set out three times on that long sea voyage to India in spite of a heart murmur. While her daughters wore fashionable ladies' hats to ride a huge Indian elephant, my grandmother sported a true safari helmet.

I decided to put the fears aside and live my life as it came. Somehow I would be given the strength I needed, when I needed it. Best of all, Neil could always make me laugh, even when I was furious with him. He had a way of pointing out something ridiculous about any situation.

One evening, Neil was washing the supper dishes in our tiny crammed apartment. I heaved a sigh as I saw him turning my new electric frying pan upside down in the sink, completely ruining it. He in turn was visibly irritated by what he called my "capacity for creating a mess" in our tiny space.

Suddenly Aretha Franklin's voice came on the radio. Both of us stopped what we were doing, came to the sofa, and sat side by side, enthralled, lifted completely out of the personal and political tensions that characterized so much of our lives at that time.

At her death, there was an outpouring around the world in celebration of her life. In an interview with *Rolling Stone* magazine, civil-rights leader John Lewis singled out Franklin's moral power. "She had the capacity and ability to help move us closer to what Dr. King called 'the beloved community'... where we could lay down the burden of hate and separation and move just a little bit closer. She lifted us and inspired us."

Ms. Franklin had travelled across America as a teenager with Martin Luther King, and also Jesse Jackson, who was present at her funeral. Her 1967 recording of the song Respect became an anthem for civil rights and feminism. Her 1972 live performances at the New Temple Missionary Baptist Church in Los Angeles were captured in a double album that stands as the biggest selling live gospel music album ever.

That album prompted the magazine *Billboard* to write, "These concerts rank as her finest hour. For eleven full minutes she lives in a state of grace, as she sings to the Lord, letting his light and his love fill her body, and then sending it pouring out into the microphone placed inches from her face and into the ears of the people sitting rapt before her in the pews, and those listening months later at home or in their car, for all eternity."

It was moments such as these that gave me a sense that whatever our difficulties, Neil's life and mine would be richer together than either of our lives apart. Marriage would be an on-going learning process.

While we were on holiday in Florida that first year in Montreal, I lent our apartment to Aunt Agnes so she could visit Montreal with my cousin Lydia. When we returned, I was approached by a close friend of Neil's boss, a woman who said to me, "Your aunt tells me you don't know how to cook." I was furious! It was not true that I could not cook. As a volunteer, I had been part of a team cooking meals for several hundred people. I knew how to fry eggs for one hundred hungry men building a film studio during the winter on Mackinac Island in Michigan. I had run a diet kitchen at Caux for thirty or forty hungry souls, including a former prominent German communist whose stomach had been damaged during the war.

However, it was also true that I had no idea how to cook consistently for one hungry male with strong likes and dislikes, apart from making sure his favourite pickles were always on the table. He had definite ideas about food being hot, promptly on the table at 6:30, with pickles firmly in their place. I had never cooked for two, and the first time guests came to dinner was nearly a disaster.

Then I saw an ad in a local paper for a gourmet cooking course and signed up. It was a stroke of good luck, especially when Neil announced to me one Saturday that he had invited Helen Rochester, the *Gazette* food critic, and her husband for supper. Helen complimented me on the sauce for the steak I served. In fact the sauce came out of a package. Maybe that was her sense of humour at play. It turned out to be an enjoyable evening of conversation and laughter.

When just the two of us were dining, however, it was a different story. I didn't have much problem with Neil's insistence that we not talk during meals, since I had grown up as an only child, had done a lot of travelling on my own, and had been living on my own. He told me he didn't want to have to think up subjects to talk about. I, on the other hand, decided to learn the language of baseball so that we could talk about games broadcast during mealtimes, which he enjoyed. He later complimented me on my mastery of baseball.

I marvelled at the tenacity and guts of this man who went on air in Montreal not even knowing the city's major intersections such as Peel and St. Catherine. The potential for blunders on air was enormous. We had come to Montreal on the strength of his part-time job at CJAD. Every night, he was doing an editorial on a different subject. At first I held my breath. Soon I relaxed. Most of the time, this guy knew what he was doing.

When Neil got married he forgot how to cook. He did, however, have one much-cherished recipe, which quickly became a staple in our household. It was for steak. First he put the steak on the frying pan, then he slathered it with soy sauce. Next he sprinkled it lavishly with dried hot peppers. Finally he turned up the heat to high.

Each time Neil used this recipe on Somerville Avenue, the smoke detector in the front hall went off with a voice telling us to leave the house immediately. I was the one whose duty it was to find a way to silence this wailing siren so we could enjoy our meal in peace.

One Friday Neil gave out this cherished recipe on his radio show. A week later a man phoned in. "Mr. McKenty," he said, "we tried your recipe last weekend. We used to have a lot of black flies. They are all gone. We used to have a lot of nosy neighbours. They are all gone. And we nailed your steak to our barn door!"

Like many newlywed couples, we had very little money. Neil's job was just starting, and it took me four months to land a job as a researcher at *Reader's Digest*. Neil had insisted that I sell the snazzy yellow Toyota that I had bought with my Queen's Park salary. It was too expensive to maintain. This sale preserved our marriage. Later, when I realized what an erratic driver Neil was, I saw the irony in one of Neil's most hilarious radio programs, "Driving with your mate."

Over the years I was well aware that my safety and even my life were at risk due to Neil's driving. I ordered my friends the Hallwards never on any account to drive with us in Maine or in Montreal. One summer evening, however, I did agree to let Clare Hallward come along with us as we headed along the lakeshore to the West Island for a relaxed supper.

At the end of the drive out, Clare said to me, "Neil did pretty well, I thought." "Yes," I replied, "if you ignore the fact he went through one red light and two stop signs." On that occasion, I could see clearly in all directions, so there was no problem. Many times, however, when I could not see if anything might be coming towards us, I had to trust my sixth sense as we navigated corner after corner.

As well as the counselling, and the sale of my car, I often say that what saved our marriage was the fact that Neil's salary included quite a few perks. We found ourselves eating at some of the nicest restaurants in the city. During the worst of the winter we were able to head for two weeks in Barbados at a resort run by a man who advertised with CJAD, had a wife in Montreal and, with the full knowledge of his wife, an attractive mistress in Barbados. We enjoyed meals cooked out of doors over a deep pit, and the most memorable dance of our lives on an open-air floor with the stars shining over our heads.

We were also given tickets to one of the early, glorious shows of the Cirque du Soleil. I was getting a real inkling of the creative talent that was emerging in Montreal. One night as we sat in a Greek restaurant on Duluth Street, I saw a pair of feet walk by the window at the level of my forehead. It was a man on stilts, out for a stroll on the summer evening. Later we joined the crowds watching a juggler at the Old Port.

Of course we spent many satisfying evenings at the Old Port. We wandered along the artists' street full of pedestrians, too narrow for cars, looking at watercolours and prints of local artists. Then we would stop for a leisurely meal in one of the alluring restaurants, followed by a stroll along the waterfront.

I say all this saved our marriage but the fact remains that underneath the daily struggles was a deep determination on my part to make this work, to honour the meant-to-be quality of our meeting on that dance floor.

I grew up in my early years with people who were not quitters. My grandfather had laboured with great persistence to get his family out of poverty, holding down two jobs most of his life, investing in real estate. Mother had grown up in a large house and that is what she had pictured for Neil and me. Yet ironically she had not wanted me to marry a son of one of the wealthy Toronto families. "Too worldly," she said. Did she picture me living alone in a mansion? What can you do about mothers! The great thing was that we now lived in separate cities. I could go back to Toronto to stay with her and have a truly happy visit without having to conform to her ideas. She agreed that the distance was a good thing; this way she didn't have to worry about why we weren't coming every Sunday to have dinner with her.

When Neil and I visited her, I only allowed Neil and my mum four days together at a time. It worked. There were no blowups. And I was truly grateful she wasn't listening to his radio show. She would have been startled to say the least.

Our lives expanded in new ways. Neil was given a chance to do the morning open-line show at CJAD. Increasingly, I felt cooped up in a nine-to-five job within four walls at *Reader's Digest*. Then, in 1973, Mr. and Mrs. Mitsui, founding heads of a high school in Japan, came to Montreal on a visit. They were interested in exploring the possibility of bringing *Reader's Digest* to Japan. During my three-week visit to Japan to view the Ontario pavilion for Expo 1970, I had stayed with them, having first met them when I volunteered with MRA in Europe.

The senior editor of *Reader's Digest* was so impressed with my connection that he immediately gave me a new assignment working on their forthcoming book, *Explore Canada*. I was sent to historic Quebec City for three days, all expenses paid.

I was also asked to edit a story about two sisters who had grown up on the edge of the Plains of Abraham and became best-selling children's authors. I went to Outremont to talk to one of them, Suzanne Martel. It was the beginning of a whole new adventure.

Suzanne had written a book for each of her six sons. Her sister, Monique Corriveau, had written a book for each of her ten children, writing at the kitchen table, with one child anchored on the clothesline. Their father was the Clerk of Quebec City, and he would march up and down during dinner, reading heroic stories from his library of six hundred books. As children, Suzanne and Monique fell in love with Kipling's India. In the attic of their home, they created forty imaginary characters whom they could summon at will out of the walls: fierce pirates, dancing girls, elephant boys and marching soldiers. By the time they were eight and twelve, they were writing their own stories.

Catharine McKenty, literary agent for Suzanne Martel, Quebec children's author, 1976

Suzanne asked me to be her literary agent and sort out what had happened to the bestseller, *The City Under Ground*, when her New York editor died. She and her husband, Maurice, a corporate lawyer, opened the door to a whole new role of publishers, contracts and book fairs. I spent a summer reading children's books. By the end of the summer, the sky was bluer and the grass greener. That winter, I went to the Salon du Livre. I collected every new Quebec children's book from the publishers, packed them in a suitcase and boarded the train to Toronto. I sold them to bookstores and libraries in Toronto. I discovered the thrill of being an entrepreneur and earned enough money to visit my mother every two months. Several other Quebec authors hired my services.

Working in another language opened up a whole other side of my personality. A francophone told me she was happier in English; I felt the same about French, although I admit I usually turned the cornflakes box around. When I was four years old, someone taught me to say, "Parlez-vous français?" I still remember the delight when a young woman answered me in a stream of fascinating syllables. I wish every child could discover languages as a delight, not a threat.

On another occasion Neil and I went to Quebec City. We visited the art gallery on the edge of the Plains of Abraham. Afterwards we strolled along the edge of the Plains, chatting as we walked. A small boy, about ten years old, came up to us. "Mr. McKenty, I recognize your voice waves. May I introduce my parents?" An enjoyable conversation followed.

We also attended the wedding of John Fleming and Claudine Roy in Quebec City on August 27, 1977. The festivities began the night before with a reception on the edge of the Plains of Abraham. After the reception, Neil and I strolled down to the National Assembly and were able to slip into the balcony for the final reading of Bill 101 and its passage into law.

Neil defended Bill 101 on his radio show, to the fury of some of his right-wing listeners. He felt that by protecting the French language, the bill helped to solidify Quebec's place within Canada. It was a position he never wavered from.

When we visited Prince Edward Island, we were fascinated to see the room where the delegates from the British North American colonies of Nova Scotia, New Brunswick and the Province of Canada hammered out the details of Canada's Confederation. In 1864, delegates had gathered to consider forming a Maritime Union of New Brunswick, Prince Edward Island and Nova Scotia, but Sir John A. Macdonald arrived on the steamer *Queen Victoria* with a boatload of lobster and champagne to "crash the party" and introduce a larger vision that would include all of Canada.

In the 1970s, I was greatly enjoying both my own work and the life of a media wife. We were invited to all kinds of events: the Irish ball, the annual celebrations in honour of Great Montrealers, dinners and CJAD parties. Neil had developed his own unique style of open-line. There was rarely a guest in the studio, but his producer arranged short phone interviews with top experts on the day's topic at the beginning and end of the show. A doctor told me Neil had educated a whole city. It is still a delight to meet young people who grew up hearing Neil's voice as their mothers listened to him. A young woman told me that she got a liberal education listening to him, unlike what she got at school.

I remember one young mother phoning in to CJAD who was having trouble coping with rambunctious twins. An older woman called in and said, "Hang in there, this time in your life doesn't last forever; you'll make it." It was immensely human and real. When Neil did a program on babies, a young woman phoned in laughing. "I haven't had my baby yet but I'm expecting it soon." Weeks later she phoned in again to say, "My baby was born with a cleft chin, which will mean some painful operations." Neil got her phone number and kept in touch with her. Years later she sent him a picture of a lovely bride at her wedding, her chin now normal. I felt privileged to have witnessed the strong connection between Neil and his listeners.

Purchase of a House on Somerville Avenue

Once Neil was in full swing with CJAD, we decided the moment had come to buy a house. Our real estate agents, Brian and Joan McGuigan, spent three hours with us that first meeting, an impressive start to our friendship. Then Joan drove me around the neighbourhoods of Notre-Dame-de-Grâce and Westmount looking at houses for sale.

Joan phoned excitedly one morning. "There is a house coming on the market in two days that you just have to see." We were due to leave on holiday the next day, but with twelve hours to spare, off we went with Brian and Joan.

It was love at first sight, to the satisfaction of the McGuigans. This was the original farmhouse on Somerville Avenue in Westmount, part of Victoria Village. Our future neighbour, eighty-year-old Mrs. Pettingill, had been born in the house. She remembered her grandfather walking from Ottawa with a cow so that his grandchildren could have fresh milk.

The house had been refurbished by four young men. One of them intended to live in it, but his wife refused. "Too difficult to cope with," she said.

When I opened the back door, there were three apple trees, a patch of rhubarb and a small black squirrel turning somersaults of pure joy. I felt I was being given back my childhood farm. No matter that neither Neil nor I could stand up straight in the basement without hitting our heads. It contained a root cellar built into the earth, where I could store fruit and vegetables. With twelve hours remaining before we left on vacation, there was no time to check the roof or the drains.

Neil wrote a deposit cheque that same evening. We were lucky. Due to all the talk of Quebec's separation from Canada, real estate prices had dropped through the floor.

The day after we moved in, Brian McGuigan was out in the garden with his large electric lawn mower, attacking the long grass with some difficulty, accompanied by Neil. I said to Joan, "I'll make us a cup of coffee."

Under an apple tree in the garden of the new house on Somerville Avenue, 1974

I put the kettle on the stove and turned the switch.

Suddenly all the lights went out and there was total silence out in the garden. We'd blown a fuse. A higher voltage was clearly needed. Fortunately, according to our contract, the sellers were required to redo the wiring. The next day Neil bought a used manual lawn mower at the Salvation Army store. From then on he happily walked up and down as the sweet smell of mown grass filled the air.

Our extra furniture was taken out of storage. No matter that the bedroom cupboards were barely a foot wide. "You can buy armoires," Joan had said blithely. I went out into the country to do just that and found a beauty. A driver helped me bring it to town on the back of his truck.

What do you know, it wouldn't go up the stairs. So we placed it in the dining room, which was really a few square feet at the back of a single long ground floor room. There it stayed for the next thirty-seven years, a convenient hiding place for all sorts of stuff. We bought a sturdy, rather homely dining room table for thirty-five dollars from a young family across the street that was moving out.

Brian and Joan couldn't help laughing at what a pair we were for having purchased a house with no time for inspection, but the location was ideal: Neil could walk to CJAD and I had a job at nearby *Reader's Digest*. For us it was perfect.

The low-ceilinged living room proved so relaxing that Neil took to having naps on my grandmother's six-foot long sofa. Visitors also found the room quite soothing. Soon my mother arrived with a generous cheque that allowed us to cancel the mortgage. I discovered later she told her maid this house was too small.

Halloween

When Halloween came that first year on Somerville Avenue, I saw a whole other side of my husband. He went out shopping for the Halloween candy then placed it in a big box on a chair just inside the front door. He had also acquired a Snoopy mask for himself and a cat mask for me.

We agreed to have an early supper at five o'clock and were just starting to eat when the doorbell rang. Neil immediately got up, put on his mask, and went to answer it. He doled out candy to each of the five children standing there. A few minutes later, the doorbell rang again. There was a small girl holding out her basket, with her mother discretely in the background. When the little girl saw Neil, she put her hand over her mouth to stop herself laughing. She stood staring for a full minute before she burst out, "I didn't know Snoopy lived here!" Her mother finally led her away, hardly concealing her own amusement.

All evening the doorbell rang with groups of children from nearby Notre-Dame-de-Grâce neighbourhood and some adults out for an evening of fun. Neil barely managed to get any supper into him, as he responded to each doorbell. It was nearly eleven-thirty before his generous supply of small chocolate bars and other candy ran out. We finally locked the door and turned out all the downstairs lights.

Neil enjoyed connecting with children. In one of my favourite photographs of him, he is cheering on eight-year-old Andrew Hallward-Driemeier, wearing a plastic Little League batter's hat, as he races for home plate after hitting a home run. Neil had given Andrew, John and Clare's grandson, his first baseball bat.

I sometimes imagined Neil as a magnificent Irish race horse. If he were startled or thrown off his feed, he would rear up, hooves flying, creating a commotion, what I called 'uproar.' Once safely into the starting gate and the bell rung, he would plunge into a flat-out gallop to the finish line.

I saw myself as a companion horse to this Irish racer with the impossible job of keeping him calmed down before every race. Much later, a friend said to me, "I think there are two race horses in the family." I was hitting my own stride.

Mercifully, Neil never vented the full strength of his anger on me. He had a protective instinct towards me and also compassion towards people who were vulnerable. I believe this is often a characteristic of someone who is bipolar. It led to his involvement with Nazareth House for the homeless, Benedict

Labré house, and work with Mohawk elders Ron and Sheila Boyer and Kevin Deer of Kanesatake.

Neil had a feisty side to his personality that led him happily into every dogfight going through his radio show. While we were courting, he had applied for jobs in publishing and print journalism. I pictured a rather professional life ahead. It was not to be. Whether it was the seal hunt, the free trade debate, or abortion, Neil was in the middle of it. People would sometimes come up at a party and expect me to explain his views. I learned to accept that we were two different people, and I neither had to defend nor change him.

From the time he was a student, Neil was interested in law. As an eight-year-old, he had followed closely the accounts of the kidnapping of the Lindbergh baby in 1932. Whenever he had a chance he would go to Peterborough by bus to spend the day at the courthouse, watching a trial. He flirted briefly with the idea of becoming a lawyer. Then his attraction to the Jesuits intervened. Each time we went on a trip to London, England, for work or pleasure, he would spend hours at the Old Bailey courthouse, watching the murder trials. I went with him once and was fascinated by the judges in their wigs, the orderliness of the whole procedure. We saw the trial of a man who tried to throttle his wife by grabbing her neck from behind.

Then of course how could he resist going down to cover the Watergate trials. Sure enough he met John Ehrlichman (who later went to prison) and discussed with him whether such a crime could happen in Canada. Then somehow he managed to get accredited to a Ronald Reagan press conference. He asked the President a carefully crafted question that visibly annoyed him.

During one cold winter, we heard that the Ville Marie Social Services were short four thousand Christmas baskets.

Corporate donations had dropped. George Balcan told the story on his early morning show. Neil said to me, "Shall we try and do something about this?" At ten o'clock he featured the story on his open-line show. I began phoning our neighbours. The first person to call in to CJAD was Gerard Fellerath. He and his wife, Gail, owned the Folklore store near us on Sherbrooke Street. They had met in the Peace Corps. Gerard said, "We'll open up a depot in our store." Immediately, the francophone superintendent from an apartment building in the East End of Montreal called CJAD to say that he would start a depot. A woman from the northern part of the city offered to drive people to the nearest depot. Calls flooded in from every corner of the city. The lines were blazing, a phrase that became Neil's signature.

Stoph Hallward, a grade school student, volunteered to collect food with his friend, Roddy Quinlan. He recalls that Neil's efforts set off a chain reaction throughout the city. "Neil McKenty stood out among my parents' friends when I was growing up. It was exciting to know someone I could hear on the radio, but when I think back on it, he never sounded any different hosting his own show than he did challenging my family in friendly banter around the dinner table. His being so himself was probably what gave me the confidence to call him on his show, once. My friend Roddy and I, who were probably eleven or twelve, decided to join the effort and went door-to-door in our neighbourhood collecting canned food. It was an easy sell and everyone gave generously."

At noon, Neil came off the air and we drove down to Ville Marie headquarters where we were met by a social worker, tears streaming down her face. "I've never seen anything like it," she said. Another neighbour, Marielle Wertheimer arrived at our door with a box of groceries, the most nourishing she could find. Gerard and Gail Fellerath drove a truckload of donated food to the depot. That Christmas, thanks to Neil, four thousand families were fed.

Later, a listener in Vermont said to me, "Neil gave Montreal a heart." In fact, the heart was always there. In the dark and cold of winter, it had shown itself.

I had thought that, as long as Neil was fully engaged in work he loved and was good at, he would be fine. What was troubling was that during the mid-1970s, Neil's outbursts of anger towards me, usually about minor stuff, became more and more frequent. I often left the house on an excuse, just to escape.

Neil describes this period in his memoir:

> Beneath the outward success and excitement of my radio work, there began to emerge an inner anxiety and agitation. It displayed itself in bursts of anger at home with Catharine and at work with my colleagues, as though just beneath my placid exterior there was a pool of rage like glowing lava waiting to erupt. At the station...I found it more stressful to talk to my colleagues than to talk to listeners on air." He added, "More and more I was retreating inside my armoured tank, desperately trying to give the impression that I didn't care...I was becoming increasingly uncomfortable in my own skin.

It is clear to me that during these years, Neil was fully comfortable only when he felt in control. This is a familiar pattern, I'm told, with children of alcoholics.

Neil could also be dictatorial at times. I remember arranging with my mum to travel down to Quebec City to explore. "I want to know when you're coming back!" he demanded in no uncertain terms. On the other hand, he could also be encouraging and supportive. In 1980, when Mum landed in the hospital with a leg infection, Neil went to see her in Toronto and they had a relaxed chat. Hospital visiting was something Neil had always enjoyed, even when he was in the Jesuits.

To help her legs heal, Neil suggested I take Mum to Florida for a week with family members of her choice. She invited Aunt Agnes and Val Fleming, with her sister Leone. They came from England to be with us. Aunt Helen joined us.

I arranged all the flights to Orlando airport, where Bob and Patsy Fleming had agreed to meet us. When we arrived, they were nowhere in sight. With two senior citizens and two Europeans in my charge, I went into action, locating wheelchairs and attendants for Mum and Aunt Agnes, navigating the trip through customs, and leading everyone to the taxi stand. I was aware that Mum was seeing a side of me that she had never known. "This is the first time I've seen you in full swing!" she exclaimed in amazement. I chuckled inwardly, pleased to discard her image of me as the slow dish washer.

A year after our trip to Florida, I talked to Mum on the phone. She wasn't feeling very well. Apparently she had stayed up all night vomiting. In the morning she called Aunt Ev, who urged her to go to the hospital by ambulance. Mum refused, so Aunt Ev drove her to the hospital. I talked to Aunt Ev who said to me, "Don't come yet." Then I had a sudden phone call from her. "I think you'd better come immediately." I caught the next flight to Toronto and as I was driving in from the airport, I suddenly knew that Mum had gone and that I wouldn't see her again. When I saw Mum's body at the hospital, I thought, "She is not here." The nurse asked me if I wanted to spend a little time sitting beside my mum, but I said no.

That night when I stood alone in Mum's apartment, I was about to break down totally. Then the Halleluiah Chorus broke into my consciousness. I'll never forget it.

Together as a family we created a beautiful ceremony for Mum at Timothy Eaton Memorial Church and she was buried in the same grave as Dad in Mount Pleasant Cemetery. The following days were full of decisions, including the closing of Mum's apartment and the sale of her furniture. Regretfully I left Toronto and returned to a daily life in Montreal with none of the wonderfully encouraging phone conversations with my mother.

It was a time of loss in the family. Having lost Mum without having said good-bye, I was privileged to spend the last five days of Aunt Agnes' life in her room at Aunt Ev's apartment. She said to me, "This must be difficult for you." I said, "No, because you're so peaceful."

"Bring me my false teeth, I've something important to tell you." I did as she asked, then she said, "I feel a spirit of joy and laughter being given, and it's been missing for a long time."

It was quite clear to me that spirit was coming from the next world. For an hour, my cousin Bob Fleming and I sat close to her bed and told all the funny stories we could think of, laughing our heads off. A few hours later, after we had gone home, she slipped peacefully away into that next world.

I had grown up in a close-knit, strictly Protestant family. Sunday after Sunday, from the time I was quite small, I sat beside my mother in the family pew at Timothy Eaton Memorial Church, where my grandfather had been the first steward. I remember the soaring soprano voice of Jean Pengelly, singing, "I know that my Redeemer Liveth."

In second year university, my childhood beliefs came crashing down when we studied Descartes' "I think, therefore I am." Soon there were so many thoughts buzzing around in my head that I wasn't even able to listen fully to a symphony concert.

Early in our marriage, I had sat next to Neil Sunday after Sunday in the pew of the Catholic Church near our home, Ascension of Our Lord. Only "Catholics in good standing" were welcome at the Eucharist, which made me indignant at first. Then I heard a sentence in the mass, "Only say the word and I shall be healed," and thought, "That's for me." From then on I was content and trusted that in some way that I could not yet understand, the conflicts and confusions in my life would gradually find resolution.

I will never forget the first time I found myself with Neil in a roomful of Montreal Catholics who all knew each other. I felt like a fish out of water, especially when one of them, a nun, said, "We hope you'll be happy with us." Immediately I felt claustrophobic. Then I realized that I only had to relate to one person at a time. I relaxed.

MEETING JOHN MAIN

Neil expressed a growing sense that something was missing in our lives. We both had work we loved, a solid marriage and by now a comfortable home. CJAD had provided Neil with a car. In 1977, he talked to a Jesuit friend who said, "There is someone who has come to town whom you should meet. Have you ever heard of John Main?" Father Main was an Irish monk who had just arrived in Montreal at the invitation of Bishop Crowley to create a safe space especially for Anglo-Montrealers at a time when so many were leaving the province. It was two years before Neil did anything, but one day in 1979 he made an appointment to see Father John. To Neil's surprise, the conversation centered not on spiritual matters, but on Neil's work fundraising for the Jesuits. (Neil tells his version of what happened in his biography of John Main, *In the Stillness Dancing*.) Neil was impressed.

John Main, O.S.B., founder of the Christian
Meditation Centre in Montreal ("the Priory")

Father John had started a meditation centre at the old Décarie house on Vendôme Avenue to teach a way of prayer that he called Christian Meditation. He himself had first learned to meditate with a Hindu Swami in Malaya when he was with the British Oversea Service as a young officer. Later, as headmaster at a school in Washington, D.C., he had rediscovered the hidden tradition from the earliest centuries of Christianity. Fr. John sent Neil home with a few tapes to listen to. He told us the beginner's group was full. In fact, I think he suspected that this particular former Jesuit might be a handful, so we were placed in the advanced group on Tuesday night.

On a cold winter night in 1979, I dutifully walked along Sherbrooke Street and up Vendôme with Neil to the Décarie house. After dumping our coats and boots we gathered in a small, low-ceilinged living room. All conversation ceased the moment people crossed the threshold. Our host sat silently in his chair at the front of the room.

I found myself with a mixed group of strangers, sitting on a lumpy old sofa with sprung springs that had been bought from the Salvation Army for $25.00. I could barely keep myself from sliding down toward the middle.

Fr. John, a tall man with an Irish accent, noticed my discomfort and said, "You can sit on the floor if you want." I did so immediately. I had no idea what I was doing. "The sooner I get out of here the better," I thought. Lacking the beginner's introduction to meditation on Mondays, I had no idea what to expect. I found this whole procedure a bit exasperating. Coming from a Northern Irish Protestant family, I had never met a Catholic monk and wasn't sure I wanted to know one now. I was thoroughly enjoying most aspects of my life as the wife of a media star. However, I thought that anything that would settle down my husband would be a good thing.

Promptly at eight o'clock, Fr. John began to speak. You could hear a pin drop. Halfway through, I realized that I was hearing a depth of spirituality that rang completely true, reminiscent of that of my beloved Granny who had been involved with medical services for women in India. It was through her that I had experienced unconditional love during my childhood. Echoes of her spirituality were integrated with a fresh language that kept me listening intently.

The teaching itself was so simple. All you had to do was repeat a prayer word or what is called a mantra for twenty minutes or so from the beginning of your meditation to the end. Simple, or so I thought. The mantra recommended was "Maranatha," the oldest known Christian prayer found at the end of the first Letter of Paul to the Corinthians, Chapter 16, Verse 22. It was in Aramaic, the language spoken at the time. Apparently its roots went much further back to the Sumerian language. All one had to do was repeat this word, forget the meaning, and listen to it as pure sound.

I did my best, but after a few minutes I found that I was thinking of what to eat for supper, or how I was going to keep sitting still. My nose itched and my foot went to sleep. The triviality of the thoughts that kept racing through my mind was embarrassing. Like Stephen Leacock's horse, my thoughts went racing off madly in all directions.

I was stubborn enough to keep on trying. "Any fool ought to be able to say one simple word for twenty minutes," I thought. In fact, children often find it more natural than adults. I concluded that I was likely the world's worst meditator. I found it uncomfortable to be in a group. I was on the verge of giving up when I heard Fr. John say, "You're on the way, so you might as well continue." That sounded manageable. And I was riveted by his insight that "we are made for a limitless expansion of spirit." It brought me back to that childhood experience of the summer evening in my grandmother's farm home when I was communing with that magnificent elm tree outside my bedroom window. I remembered the sound of summer insects filling the air and the smell of petunias wafting up from the flower beds below.

Neil and I continued to go every Tuesday night. The following year, in 1980, when the community was given a much larger house on Pine Avenue, Neil suggested we go on Friday evenings for mass and meditation, as well as on Sunday morning. This was a drastic change in the schedule of our lives. I was furious at the time but I went, cursing under my breath. Given a choice, I would have chosen a cocktail party over Friday night mass.

After a time, I noticed that a different rhythm had entered our lives. Neil's driving improved. Explosions were fewer. I noticed that my relationships with people were changing. At times it felt as though my whole inner landscape was shifting. The deep inner anxiety I had often felt in groups, as far back as childhood, began to loosen its grip.

I was also delighted with Fr. John's ability to deal with my complicated, bipolar husband. Neil would formulate the most challenging and complicated questions he could think of. One time Fr. John commented at the end of his talk, "You asked an interesting question last week, Neil, in spite of yourself." I cheered. Another time, however, Fr. John made the effort to call us at home to ask, "Did I fully answer your question?" We were privileged to be part of a time when Fr. John was developing the fuller articulation of his insights.

The move to the Pine Avenue house in 1980, formerly the home of the McConnell family, provided a new setting for the spaciousness of Fr. John's vision. Gradually, the pattern of our week began to solidify, this time with my full agreement. We were going to Tuesday night meditation, five o'clock meditation and mass on Friday to wrap-up the work week, then Sunday mass. Fr. John had a beautiful voice and his singing at the monks' nightly Compline was lovely. The people who turned up on these occasions were a motley crew, "like the inside of a Montreal bus," as Fr. John described it. They also included Prime Minister Pierre Elliott Trudeau, who lived across the street.

Fr. John was a commanding, almost medieval, figure as he came down the staircase in his monastic robes. Some people, including me, felt quite intimidated. Then one Sunday morning we arrived for mass a few minutes earlier than usual. Fr. John greeted us in his shirt sleeves, muttering something about "washing the windows, you know." We stood talking in the sunshine. Years later I realized that monks don't wash windows on Sunday. He had made an effort to appear approachable for my sake and for others like me.

At the monastery on Pine Avenue, people had a sense of coming into a family, a family that opened its doors to the whole city. This was often demanding for those who lived there. Some days, Fr. John didn't get to eat breakfast before 11 a.m. But a bond was created that included those of us living in our own homes.

Meditation affected each person differently and we were advised to have no expectations. This was good advice. I was thoroughly unprepared for the changes that continued to take place in my life. I had a million questions but it never occurred to me to talk to Fr. John personally. Once I asked about breathing during a group session. He replied with a twinkle, "By all means, keep breathing." Then he relented and told us there were helpful exercises we could do. One of them involved lying on the floor. That was too much for me, so I muddled along as best I could. At one point, someone told me the ideal way was to say the whole of the mantra on the in breath and listen to it on the out breath. I've heard of variations since, but I tried this and nearly choked. Much later one of the nuns who was part of the community, Sr. Camille Campbell, said the same thing to me, "Try it, it's easy. Your ribs will hurt a bit at first, but you can do it." And I did.

Learning to breathe from my stomach turned out to be one of the best things I could have done for my own health, but I was a slow learner.

Through the monastery, which was officially called a Priory, we made many new friends. We occasionally stayed for the weekend. On the first weekend, we were shown to our rooms. Neil stayed in the main building with the monks, while a rather dismal-looking visiting nun escorted me up the hill in the pouring rain to the coach house set aside for the women. Another weekend, we became friends with Marie Foley, Manager of the Nielsen Gallery in Boston and her writer-philosopher husband, Andrew. It was a rich part of our life and an important balance to the fast pace of the rest of it.

Through meditation, an inner balance was being restored, a shift from the need to be non-stop doing toward simply being. I still retained my own territory as I found my life once again realigning itself with an energy greater than my own, the energy of love at the heart of the universe.

After three years of going to mass at the Priory every Sunday, it occurred to me that I would feel quite comfortable becoming a Catholic. I wasn't the least interested in structures. Whenever I went back to Toronto I happily attended the Protestant service at Timothy Eaton Memorial Church where I grew up. I loved the Catholic Church, with its roots in so many countries. After a visit to Mexico, I told my aunt, "Even the goats go to church there!"

Meditation itself was becoming more and more important to me. Father John spoke about an experience beyond words. That was also a good description of the sacrament of reconciliation, created for me by Fr. John in the chapel at the Pine Avenue house. Sr. Gertrude McLaughlin told him I had never had proper instruction in Catholicism, that I had simply fired twenty questions at her.

One of these questions was, "What's all this about obedience?" Her reply was, "Well, as the Duke of Wellington once said, 'To obey exactly is not to obey at all.'" Later I figured the Duke probably said no such thing, but it was a good answer.

During the ceremony, at the moment when Fr. John placed a drop of oil on my forehead, I felt his hand trembling. For an instant I found myself in another realm of consciousness, out of time. In that moment my rich Protestant heritage and my Catholic experience came together in a single whole. To this day, I call myself a hybrid. I feel comfortable in any of the churches I find myself in at weddings or funerals or regular service.

Over time, I had come to trust Fr. John as a friend held at a distance. I rarely had a conversation with him, as I guarded my hard-won sense of personal autonomy that had come at a high cost. I sensed that it would be too easy to put him up on a pedestal.

Never again was I going to be taken over by a guru, or turn my life over to a group. I had a sense of a small piece of spiritual territory under my feet. It might have been small but it was mine. And so, when I sat at the long dining room table at the Priory, I deliberately sat at the opposite end of the table from Fr. John. There were empty seats in between and he beckoned me closer. I moved half-way down. Roaring with laughter because he knew what I was avoiding, he insisted I move closer. I did and spent the whole meal talking to the woman next to me. A small incident but indicative of this cautious relationship.

Tuesday after Tuesday, I listened to Fr. John give talks, partly alert for any false note, but mainly because a sentence or two would leap out. I was hearing things I had heard all my life that were making sense in a new way.

I remember him saying that for a long time the Church has placed too great an emphasis on sin. In meditation, we discovered that we were loved, that we were loveable. He viewed Christianity as a revelation for the whole of humanity, not the possession of a few. And yet he was authentically Benedictine and Roman Catholic. On one memorable occasion, the Dalai Lama kept his whole entourage waiting in order to meditate with Fr. John and his community.

There was a side to his personality that some people found difficult to live with, but as he grew older, a mellowing and self-awareness took hold. He had loved his early life at Trinity College in Dublin, going to the racetrack and enjoying his friendships with all kinds of people. His choice to become a monk was a difficult one because he had had to leave all that behind. Because of this I trusted him. I remember him saying, "Our greatest sin would be to not live life to the fullest." I could buy that. There was no pressure to arrive anywhere or to produce results.

In my years with Moral Re-Armament in Europe, I had experienced enormous pressure within the group to produce results. We were supposed to be "saving the world for democracy." In some cases, families were needlessly neglected and individual talents unused and unrecognized. Our personal needs were subordinated to the task at hand. It was an attitude often necessary under war-time conditions but it took a very high a toll in civilian life. Burnout showed up in various forms, and eventually many of the group dropped out. In contrast, I felt no pressure during those years with Fr. John.

Challenging Times

In 1980, Aunt Ev wrote an encouraging letter to me about my marriage. In it she said, "Your relationship is unfolding in the storm and the sunshine." How prophetic those words would prove to be. Not only was my husband a thunderstorm of energy, but the political climate in Quebec had been heating up for years.

How could I forget the shock of the first election to power of the Parti Québécois in 1976 under René Lévesque? The garden of Terry Mosher, the *Gazette*'s cartoonist, was kitty-corner to ours. The *Gazette* carried perhaps his most famous cartoon. "Take a Valium" for all his readers to both chortle and wince at.

The serenity of meditation was interrupted by the uproar leading up to the first Referendum on Quebec's sovereignty. During the tense days leading up to that first

Referendum, Neil had kept a conversation going on his open-line show between people of differing views. A third of his listeners were francophones. René Lévesque, the separatist Premier of Quebec, was a guest, as was the Prime Minister of Canada, Pierre Elliott Trudeau. I hadn't realized that Lévesque had been a Liberal who had left the party in 1968 to found his own party, the Parti Québécois. Neil had considerable respect for the way he kept his followers back from violence. A lawyer friend also told me that if anyone else had been in Neil's job, there could have been violence. When de Gaulle made his fist-pumping proclamation, "Vive le Québec libre!" Neil skillfully mitigated the extreme reaction of listeners.

While Neil was on air, I was fully involved with a group getting out the vote against separatism, under the leadership of Sally Drummond and Louise Agar. "They were our political godmothers," Nicole Forbes said to me in a recent conversation. "I learned how to do pointage, door-to-door canvassing. It was lots of fun, as well as hard work." Margaret Cuddihy, John Pepper and Richard French were also part of that team.

I was assigned four polls. Polio survivor Barbara Whitely took on one of the most physically demanding polls, navigating up steps with her walker.

I honestly believed that the French language would be better protected if Quebec remained in Canada. Now children all across the country were hearing it in train and airport announcements. My niece in Ontario had received such a good grounding in school she was now teaching in French.

The Referendum in 1980 was followed by a tense election for a new government. Bernie St. Laurent had joined CJAD in January 1977 as a political reporter covering the National Assembly. He became one of Neil's most respected colleagues. During the lead-up to the 1981 election everyone in the anglophone community was convinced that Claude Ryan of the Liberal Party would win.

Bernie told me in a recent conversation, "Ryan, as leader of the Liberal Party in Quebec, had just been on the winning side of the 1980 Referendum. I had been out reporting in the Quebec City area. I said to Neil, 'Come along with me to an east end shopping centre,' in that city. He took one side, I took the other. We met soon after. 'Jesus Christ, Bernie, the PQ is going to win!' Neil said in a state of total shock. We both realized that people in general didn't much like Ryan. It had actually been Pierre Elliott Trudeau with his speeches who had turned the tide of the Referendum." Who can ever forget the electricity in the Paul Sauvé Arena in Montreal: "Je suis Pierre Elliott Trudeau!"

I told Bernie I had just been reading the article about him in the *Montrealer* of May 1, 2008. "You had an incredible career, Bernie," I said. "I was lucky," he replied,

> I find politics fascinating. I was initiated as a boy, listening to Uncle Louie, then Prime Minister of Canada in the Fifties (Louis St. Laurent was his great-uncle). Then I talked politics with my father and grandfather in the Compton General Store they owned down in the Eastern Townships. I remember sitting around a pot-bellied stove, drinking Pepsi and analysing the latest political news. When Uncle Louis came to visit, there were reporters all over the place and the whole town turned out.
>
> My mother's idea was that I would go into the priesthood. I didn't go along with that. I got kicked out of boarding school for insubordination. Luckily, I was accepted at St. Patrick Catholic Secondary School, the only school that would take me. Then I entered Ryerson's journalism programme. I left it when I landed a job at the Sherbrooke *Record*, after

being interviewed by Conrad Black. I covered murder trials plus all sorts of other assignments.

Nick Auf Der Maur helped me to get hired by CJAD and I opened their first bureau in Quebec City. I was there for Bill 101, the Referendum, and all the other PQ initiatives. At CJAD I met Neil. I had a high respect for him because he was open to hearing opinions other than his own and considering other options. When he formed his own opinion, however, it was quite firm. I found his training impressive.

Bernie is also a mentor with the MUHC Recovery Transition Program for people with mental health or addiction issues.

The Field of Carrots

After the uproar had died down over the 1980 Referendum on Quebec's separation from Canada, I went looking for ways that anglophones and francophones could work together for the common good. Each of us matters; each of us has a gift the world needs, as urgently as the rarest plant hidden away in the rain forest. Suppose we started to look at each other in that way; suppose we listened more closely to each other, setting aside our own preconceived ideas and plans.

At a local art exhibition, I met one of the staff of La Relance, an outstanding organization in the poorest area of Montreal, dedicated to the well-being of children and families. She told me their most immediate need was a healthy snack for one hundred children who arrived at the centre without breakfast.

I was going into hospital for a hip operation so I couldn't do anything. I started praying for apples and cheese. After I emerged from the hospital I went to a funeral. Out of the blue an agriculture student said to me, "I've been offered a field of carrots. Do you know anyone who could help me pick them?" I started laughing. I had a mental picture of a field of carrots flying from the west end of Montreal to the poorest section in the east end, where the children lived. That night I phoned an assortment of friends and acquaintances.

The next day we headed for the field. A ten-year-old pushed a cardboard box along the ploughed field while I plucked carrots from the top of the furrows, holding onto my Canadian crutch for dear life. Then, one of the students said to me, "I've been loaned a truck by my grandparents who own an apple orchard." After we loaded our cars and the truck with dirty carrots we headed for the orchard.

With the help of three children, two single mothers, a set of grandparents, an enthusiastic group of students, and an unemployed film producer who supplied pitchforks, we loaded two truckloads of carrots, apples, and fresh cider.

Next came the question, "Where do we get the cheese?" I phoned a milk company that I'd been told was run by the Mafia. "Yes, we'll give you the cheese but don't ask too often." I was welcomed by a man who looked just like the Godfather. Another man with a gun on his hip helped me load a generous amount of cheese into the car.

The following day Neil and I drove down to La Relance with the trunk of the car loaded with dirty carrots. The loaded trucks arrived soon after.

Judy Stevens, founder of Share the Warmth, a food bank and community centre in Little Burgundy, heard the story and was inspired to extend her involvement further east into Sainte-Marie. Soon, lunch-time food was shipped from Share the Warmth to schools in Sainte-Marie that had kitchens of their own. Then the mothers of Sainte-Marie decided to drive out the drug dealers and pimps who were endangering their children. With the help of the police, they took over the street for a day.

All these events were the beginning of an ongoing project. The energy released in all of us through that field of carrots, and in people like us everywhere in the world, is something we haven't been able to measure. Perhaps we are just beginning to catch a glimpse of what it is to be fully human.

> "What is our fullest destiny?
> To become love in human form
> We work to enchant others
> We work to ignite life
> > To awaken presence, to enhance
> > The unfolding of being.
> All of this is the actuality of love."
> > —Brian Swimme, physicist

EXCHANGE

While Neil's radio programme *Exchange* was receiving top ratings, he said to me, "Let's create a discussion group in our home, and invite some of our friends. We'll call it *Exchange*." Next thing you knew, the doorbell started ringing every second Wednesday after supper, and a colourful mix of people began arriving.

It included a priest, an ex-priest, a divorced and remarried Catholic couple, an editor, several teachers, a couple of social workers, a former councillor and the Chairman of the United Way.

Neil had great fun lining up the guests. His idea was to have discussions that were both stimulating and provocative. I was fascinated by the figures in public life who would take time to share their ideas off the record with this small group.

Claude Ryan was a guest on more than one occasion. Neil also invited federal NDP leader Tom Mulcair, business executive Reed Scowen and provincial cabinet minister John Ciaccia. Canadian politician Warren Allmand and theologian Gregory Baum were frequent guests.

One memorable evening centred around three women from Palestine and three women from Israel. After the discussion we all ended up in the kitchen, talking our heads off over peppermint tea and biscuits. When the evening ended all too soon, there were hugs all round.

Other guests included Douglas Hall and Catherine Young, both from the Faculty of Religious Studies at McGill; Sean McEvenue, Professor of Old Testament Theology, and Christine Jamieson, Professor of Theology, both from Concordia.

Many of the discussions were anything but heavy stuff. They covered the topics from the use of the waterfront to gay marriage. They also included life issues such as the right to die, led by Pamela Bright. Patrick Dunn led a discussion on death and dying with palliative care. On occasion, members of the group were invited to lead the discussion.

Neil sat quietly in his favourite chair in the far corner of the room, throwing out a question as needed, but rarely saying much himself. If he noticed Chris Elliott, former Jesuit priest and daring mountain climber, was being unusually quiet, he would gently throw him a question. There was something about that room in the old farmhouse on Somerville Avenue that encouraged conversation and relaxation. The ceiling was low and none of the furniture was new. The long sofa and several of the wooden pieces had been in my family for two or three generations. Those evenings gave us great pleasure.

When Neil left CJAD, he continued the group with zest. My role was to cook supper, put the dishes in the dishwasher, help make the room ready, and prepare a snack for our visitors. As the months wore on, I ordered supper from our friends at the Toucheh restaurant, and did my best to stay awake. One time, however, I invited a very special guest.

On my return by train from a visit to Toronto, I had been placed in a seat next to a woman who was absorbed in her thoughts. I was tired and glad just to sit. Neither of us said a word until we were quite close to Montreal. Suddenly I thought, "I need to talk with this woman." I introduced myself. By some miracle she started to tell me a little of her story. We heard the rest at a memorable *Exchange* evening in our home.

Her name was "Twinkle" Rudberg. One evening she and her husband decided to go out to dinner. They were nearly at the restaurant when they caught sight of an elderly woman having her purse snatched by a 14-year-old boy.

Twinkle's husband stopped the car and jumped out to help. "Drive around the block, then come back to pick me up," he said to Twinkle. She did just that. When she returned, she found to her horror her husband lying dead on the sidewalk. He had been knifed by the teenager.

Through months of profound grief, she came to terms with the experience of victimhood also shared by that teenager. She decided to share the experience with others. The result was LOVE: Leave Out Violence. Its stated aim was "to reduce violence in the lives of youth and in our communities by building a team of youth who communicate a message of non-violence."

At LOVE, violence was defined as any action that causes pain: emotional, physical or social. This included domestic violence, sexual assault, sexual harassment, self-harm, different forms of bullying, fighting, gang-related violence, substance abuse, and suicide. Also included were hate crimes, racism, sexism and homophobia.

LOVE's vision all along has been to inspire youth to build a society free of fear and violence, to change themselves while also building the capacity to help others. Twinkle and her co-founders were convinced that changes in youth behaviour were best made through peer-to-peer communication.

The website of LOVE reports that "80% of our graduates report that there has been a significant decrease in their experiences with violence. 82% have completed or are in the process of completing CEGEP (2015 Alumni questionnaire)." Out of Twinkle's horrific experience, LOVE has launched programmes in Toronto, Halifax and Vancouver. Steve Sims, a member of *Exchange*, conducted a day-long event for the LOVE group in Vancouver.

We learned from Twinkle that these groups offer youth training in media arts through photography and writing, social and emotional learning, as well as leadership development in a safe setting.

I was fascinated to learn from the website that LOVE in Montreal now engages five hundred youth ages 13 to 19, all because of Twinkle's experience with that one boy.

John Main's Death

Just before Christmas 1981, we were stunned to learn that Fr. John was ill with cancer. We had seen him in a wheelchair but he had spun a tale about a war-time injury. His Irish capacity for storytelling was one of the things that we loved about him.

Father John's death from cancer at the age of 56 on December 18, 1982 was a tremendous shock. It was only then that I realized the depth of friendship we had experienced. To my surprise, it felt like losing one of my own family.

During his last hours in a coma, Neil and I said good-bye to Fr. John and promised that we would continue his work, as did many others. Neil stayed in John's room for four hours on his last day, and that night Fr. Laurence, Fr. John's successor, asked Neil to write John Main's biography.

IRELAND 1982 – 1992

WRITING THE BIOGRAPHY OF JOHN MAIN

W e both felt it was the privilege of a lifetime. Quite apart from his spiritual teaching, we had learned a lot about living from this man, often without knowing it.

In June of 1982, Neil took two weeks' vacation and we flew to London.

As we were going through security at the airport, the guard on duty looked at Neil's passport, stared at Neil for a long moment, stared at me, then shrugged his shoulders and waved us through. The guard at Heathrow airport did the same thing. While we were waiting for the airport bus into the city, Neil took another look at his passport and gave a great chortle. "I wonder who he thought you were," he said. By mistake, during a hurried packing, he had picked up his old passport, with its photo of him in full Jesuit garb.

From the Heathrow airport bus terminal, we took a cab that hustled us through the back streets of London to the Pimlico area where I had found an inexpensive bed-sit, as they were called. It came complete with a pay phone. While Neil was out interviewing some of the people who had known

Douglas Main (John Main's christened name) in his early years, I dropped copper pennies into the telephone. Neil interviewed at least sixty people during those two weeks in London.

We had been given a small address book belonging to Fr. John with forty names in it, but no other papers. Piecing this man's life together was a challenging task but I loved the detective work.

First I turned my attention to the *Hornsey Journal*, the newspaper where young Douglas had worked before his stint in the army. I looked for his byline and some of the stories he told us he had covered. There were no bylines because it was war-time, and no sign of those stories. I gave up.

My next aim was to find any of the men who had been in the special intelligence unit during the war. At seventeen, Douglas had joined a small mobile unit of British Intelligence. His job was to hone in on the signals of enemy agents still working in France. He worked from a beefed up ambulance, concentrating on the difficult task of sorting out enemy signals from the cluttered mass of airwaves. At the meditation centre, Fr. John had compared the process of focusing on a single word or mantra to the concentration on a signal.

Thanks to the discovery of Enigma, the German code machine, these signals revealed the location of enemy agents who were then captured. By chance, I discovered the location of Enigma, and went down to Bletchley Park to have a look at it. I asked so many questions about how it worked that finally the young officer in charge said to me in exasperation, "Miss, you are going to have to get clearance if I'm to tell you any more."

After three phone calls and referrals, I was able to track down one of the men from this special unit. He lived in Scotland and was able to put me in touch with another of the men, Tudor Jones, a Welsh policeman who had no phone. This man told me of long walks with young Douglas, who talked to him about a sense of spiritual calling. "It was always with him," Tudor Jones said.

During Neil's holidays the next summer, we went to Ireland where we met many of Douglas Main's family and friends. I remember sitting on the floor playing with one of Yvonne Fitzgerald's grandchildren while she told stories about her brother with all the gifts of an actress. We gained a picture of this man that was far more human than anything we had known in Montreal.

While Neil continued with conversations, I sat huddled up under a blanket in a nearby hotel while it poured rain outside, reading a stack of background books. I came across a description of one of the Main ancestors, Charles Kickham, a tall man with piercing eyes that could look right through you. I laughed out loud. This was an exact description of Fr. John, and one of the reasons I had sat at the far end of the table.

As Neil and I met more of this close-knit Irish family, I began to understand more clearly Fr. John's desire to share the sense of belonging with more people. A nephew remembered him sitting quietly in the corner during a visit home to Ireland. Soon, a whole roomful of family members began orbiting around him.

The thirty-year restriction period on army records had just expired for Douglas Main's records. We were finally able to see a copy of Douglas' honourable discharge papers. But his two army buddies confirmed by phone what we had begun to suspect. Some of Fr. John's wonderful war stories told around the fire at Pine Avenue were precisely that: fantastic tales woven by a gifted Irish storyteller. My straight-laced Methodist upbringing hadn't prepared me for the extent of the embroidery. Apparently there were no forays behind enemy lines or Paris safe-houses, just steady hard work, well behind Allied lines. The stories were in fact an art form that revealed more of the inner reality of Fr. John than the mundane facts could have, a kind of poetry of life.

Out of this experience, I wondered how much was true of the story of the Swami in Malaya, from whom he had learned to meditate. Did the Swami exist? Neil talked to several people who had been in Malaya at the time and knew Douglas. No Swami. Finally I found a judge whom we had been told to talk to. Eureka! Not only did he remember the Swami, but he had remained a member of the Pure Life Society founded by Swami Satyananda. It was now run by Mother Mangalam, who had kept the orphanage going just as the Swami had started it, with children of the four major religions of Malaya learning to live together. He had organized the first interfaith conference in Malaya after the war and was recognized as a statesman. The judge sent us a biography of the Swami, who had been killed in a car accident, and a copy of Sr. Mangalam's newsletter.

After the two weeks were up, Neil returned to CJAD. I went off for a week in Paris to stay with a friend from my days as a speech writer, Joy Gordon. I sat for some hours at the foot of the statue of the Virgin Mary in Notre Dame Cathedral, wondering about John Main. "Was this guy for real?" Gradually, the questions faded away. I knew from experience that meditation as I had learned it from Fr. John, difficult though I found it (and still do), was one of the most important discoveries of my life. To this day, I marvel at the chain of events that led to my meeting Neil and then both of us meeting John Main.

It was as though everything in Neil's life had led up to his work on the biography: his love of writing that began when he was nine years old; his training with the Jesuits to look at all sides of a question and sift out the essentials; his years of evoking a wide range of opinions on the radio and sense of what would interest a large and disparate audience; even his galloping energy allowed him to accomplish a vast amount of work in a relatively short time.

As Neil became absorbed in writing the drafts of *In The Stillness Dancing*, his spirit responded and he was happier and more fulfilled than I had ever known him to be. Our house was full of joyous energy and we were able to communicate easily back and forth. This was a very different sort of energy from the one that had sometimes erupted during his early years in radio and in the early years of our marriage. Even the tone of his voice sounded calmer on tapes that I have listened to from that period.

As Neil wrote in his memoir, he was always grateful to Father Laurence Freeman for having asked him to write that biography, and I share in that gratitude. We were also fortunate in having a fine editor for this book, Teresa de Bertodano at Darton, Longman and Todd.

For the first two years, Neil continued his radio show, returning home for lunch and four hours of intensive writing in the afternoon. I organized the research material which he would sift through at the same time as he prepared for his next day's radio show.

Once Neil got into full swing with the book, there was no looking back. I followed up on leads and read every page as it came off the battered pink and grey portable typewriter I had bought from a staff member at *Pace*. Neil preferred this old manual typewriter to the early computers. It went with us on brief holidays.

The first draft was a disaster. Neither Fr. Laurence nor I liked it much. But it was important that nothing throw Neil off track, now that he was out of the starting gate and was gathering momentum. I told Fr. Laurence, "Your job discussing the book with Neil will be harder than writing the book yourself," and Fr. Laurence proceeded with a diplomacy that kept Neil's resolve intact.

After two years of this schedule Neil finished a second draft but still was not satisfied. One evening in July 1985, he said to me, "Catharine, we need to talk. If I am going to do justice to John Main and the significance of his life and work, I need to concentrate on just doing that. I'm seriously thinking of leaving CJAD."

I was stunned. The radio show was going so well. The Friday morning special program of *Exchange*, called *What's On Your Mind?* was flooded with calls. The new ratings had just come out and *Exchange* had 76,000 listeners. How could Neil walk away from all that? I had listened in on some of the shows, something I had refused to do in the early years of our marriage, much to Neil's annoyance.

Up to this point I had been excited by the writing project. Now I began to be a bit nervous about where this whole meditation thing was taking us. After John Main's death in 1982, Neil had started an evening meditation group in our home. We had naively invited all our neighbours on Somerville Avenue to join us. One neighbour came and left immediately after the meditation, saying angrily, "This isn't what I expected." Another couple made it quite clear they were not interested and had seen too many people go right off the deep end, ending up in ashrams all over the world. At the time it had been a lesson for both of us. We reminded ourselves that John Main had friends in Washington with whom he dined and never spoke about meditation. Two of his sisters only learned about meditation when they came to his funeral in Montreal.

Sister Coté invited us to help her start a meditation group at Nazareth House, a home environment with support for people who struggle with homelessness, addictions and mental health issues. She had hoped that one or two of the street people in Montreal might benefit by meditation. However, it turned out not to be realistic for any of them. Pat Murphy had joined us and often it was just Sister Coté, Pat, Neil and me, a rewardingly small group. Yet having seen our neighbours' reaction to our invitation to meditate, I asked myself how the publication of this book and Neil leaving the radio show would affect our lives. We had been through so many upheavals.

But then I thought about the rare privilege of meeting John Main, whose teaching was the opposite of "going off the deep end." Most important was his calming effect on Neil. I gave my whole-hearted support to a decision that neither of us ever regretted.

We had supper with John and Clare Hallward and went over all the pros and cons of Neil's full-time commitment to the biography. I dropped in to see the therapist we had consulted long ago. Tobi listened and then said, "Don't ever think, no matter how things turn out, that this was a mistake." During the difficult times that were to come, I always came back to those words.

Mike Boone, the *Gazette* radio and television critic wrote in his full-page article, "Neil McKenty is about to walk away from one of Montreal's most successful radio programs... The July 26 edition of 'Exchange' will be the last time McKenty goes on the air to tell 75,000 listeners, 'The lines are blazing!'"

With what I thought was great ingenuity and foresight, but with a minimum of consultation, I booked an office service downtown for Neil. It provided a room where he could work and someone to answer his phone calls. I envisioned our home being inundated by phone calls from upset listeners who missed his voice. It was a washout. Neil loved our cozy home and was happiest typing away in his office upstairs. Most of his listeners only wanted to speak to him one more time. He admitted to me that he missed their calls, and was pleased when listeners' messages were relayed by CJAD.

Neil and I enjoyed the occasional visit with author Louise Penny and her husband Michael Whitehead, a doctor. We applauded as popularity of her books grew and grew, and stayed up until all hours reading each mystery as it came off the press.

In September 1985, we flew back to Ireland for intensive follow-up meetings with John Main's family and friends. These conversations were exhilarating stuff. But when Neil came back from a trip to Ealing Abbey in London, he was downcast. "I'm not sure there's a book." Having heard the conflicting opinions about Fr. John at Ealing Abbey, Neil had no wish to fan controversy or harm the memory of the friend we had loved. It was a puzzler.

Without Diana Ernaelsteen, there would have been no book. She had known Douglas Main in England since she was eight and he thirteen. He came as a war evacuee to her home in Welwyn Garden City in England. I cried my way through Neil's telling of her story over lunch in a little restaurant in Pimlico. I was struck by the integrity and strength of these two people in following their chosen paths: she, a doctor, and he, a monk. Both their stories have enriched my own.

Later, I spent four days on my own with Diana in Welwyn Garden City. It's a friendship I cherish. I was not surprised to discover that the Queen invested her with an Order of the British Empire for her medical work.

Talking to Douglas' sister, Yvonne Fitzgerald, I discovered that their father had become an alcoholic. Their mother had coped with him by adopting a certain vagueness. Yvonne had not wanted this mentioned in the book, for the sake of the grandchildren.

After the third draft, the book was accepted by Neil's editor in England, Teresa de Bertodano. To our consternation, the senior editor at Darton, Longman and Todd, instructed that the book be cut by thirty percent. All that research and work out the window. Thank goodness Clare and John Hallward were there with us for that difficult task. Finally I had to admit that it made the book more readable, less expensive and therefore able to reach more people. Crossroads in New York came on board to publish an American edition.

In the summer of 1987, *In the Stillness Dancing* was launched at Trinity College, Dublin. Yvonne made the arrangements. It was to be an exciting event for both Neil and me. We sat there for nearly two hours with a pile of books. Only half a dozen people showed up. Apparently there had been no publicity.

Yvonne later told us a bit sheepishly that she hadn't liked the biography. It was too honest. Later she changed her mind and admitted to me that it was the best thing ever written about her brother, whom she obviously had placed on a pedestal.

The book was reviewed by Mary McAleese, who was to become President of the Republic of Ireland, with the headline, "Best Book of 1987." She wrote:

> At a time in my own life, when I felt the deepest need for developing and growing in my prayer life, I found John Main's simple and unadorned introduction to Christian meditation exciting and effective. His biography, with the magical title, taken from a poem by T.S. Eliot, is an intriguing insight into this man of many contradictions, all unified in his love of Church and Christ...His taped talks on stillness and meditation have helped me through more than one traffic jam and more than one dark night....He is undoubtedly a great teacher on that journey from surface to self.

Neil put every ounce of his skill and passion into the portrait of John Main as we knew him. Yet he always felt he hadn't quite captured the essence of the man. Perhaps this wasn't possible with such an extraordinary subject.

Since the publication of the biography, some of the people Neil interviewed and wrote about have died. Their stories would have been lost if Neil had not responded as thoroughly as he did. I have seldom seen anyone work so hard. Often, we would stroll out for a meal at ten o'clock at night. On cold winter nights, our wonderful friends at the Toucheh restaurant in Montreal brought a hot meal right to our door. There was no body of papers and letters as there had been for Neil's biography of Ontario Premier Mitch Hepburn. At the time of his death, Fr. John was largely an unknown figure, even in Montreal, except among those whose lives he touched.

We still run into people whose lives have been affected by reading the biography. One woman had just lost her son. She walked into a downtown bookstore. "The book just jumped off the shelves at me," she said. She began meditating and the house on Pine Avenue became a reference point. A scientist from McGill told us the book "fell on the floor at her feet—it was the strangest thing." She picked it up, began reading and has been meditating ever since.

The Anglican Bishop of Virginia sent out 3500 copies of the American edition to his book club. Supportive reviews appeared on both sides of the Atlantic, as well as in Malta and Australia. A brand new printing with a portrait of Fr. John on the cover is now available from Light Messages Publishing, as well as on Amazon.

A week after Neil and I returned from the launch of *In the Stillness Dancing*, he got a call from Producer Don McGowan at CFCF television, inviting him to do an open-line morning show. "The poor man's Larry King," Don joked.

It was a three year adventure, with guests such as sex therapist Dr. Ruth and Premier René Lévesque (two weeks before his death) with a marvellous production team of young people headed by Daniel Freedman, assisted by Wendy Helfenbaum and Joan Takefman.

In Neil's view, and mine as well, his most memorable interview on CFCF television was with a man who had spent forty-two years in prison, Gilles Thibault. As a youngster he was living in a boys' home. He was arrested at the age of twelve for stealing a bicycle to go to the funeral of his mother, who had been a prostitute. One thing led to another: bank robbery, incarceration, solitary confinement, no parole. For the next forty-two years he was in and out of prison, in and out of solitary, received the lash and was assigned to cut down hanged prisoners.

One night, when he was completely at the end of his tether, unable to go on any longer, he knelt down in his cell and said one word, "Help." A feeling like ten Valiums came over him. He went to sleep and the next morning wrote a letter to a very stern judge asking for one last chance at parole.

Parole was granted. Gilles took up a normal daily life, met a lovely woman whom he married, and wrote a book, *42 ans en prison*, which was widely distributed and translated into English. His wife was waiting for him at CFCF when he came off the air, and Neil went down to talk with both of them. I watched this extraordinary interview from home. In 1990 our Christmas letter was entitled "Unforgettable Characters" and it was mostly about Gilles Thibault.

DONWOOD – MOOD SWINGS

Even though Neil was enjoying his job at CFCF-TV, his mood took a downward turn after the high of writing and publishing the John Main biography. There is no question that

I found these mood swings difficult to deal with. It is generally known now that bipolar disorder is often characterized by extreme mood swings. Since his early years of training with the Jesuits, he had had difficulty sleeping. This got worse as time went on, making him irritable around the house, except when he was fully occupied or serenely reading the newspaper in his comfy green upholstered armchair.

Finally, Neil's sleep issues came to head, and his doctor referred him to the Donwood Clinic in Toronto. We packed our bags while Neil muttered irritably about something. Once we were on the road, my own anger boiled over, and I let off a blast, of all the lousy timing. Now we were cooped up in a car for five hours, with no way to escape each other's company, on our way to a sleep clinic, of all things.

On our way home, Neil told me quietly that the psychologist had said to him, "Your wife is not helping you." At that moment I decided to do something about my own boiling anger. I invented a strategy for dealing with Neil's outbursts of irritability when there was no time for discussion. Whenever I felt anger building up in my biceps, I would walk halfway down our cellar stairs and turn myself into an imposing Japanese Sumo wrestler. I would begin punching the air over and over until the angry energy was fully released. Then I was able to go back upstairs and move on to whatever required my attention.

One day I was expecting guests for lunch. Neil arrived home from an errand five minutes before they were due to arrive. Once again, he was irritable in a way that upset me. I went down the cellar stairs, the Sumo wrestler thrashed her tense arms aggressively, and I was able to go back up to greet our lunch guests serenely, my festive mood intact.

Neil's six-week stay at the Donwood Clinic had a remarkable effect on him. I remember the drive home to Montreal. It was as though Neil was in the zone, with the traffic magically moving away from us. Because of his treatment, he got off sleeping pills entirely and was far more peaceful, at least for the time being.

Recently, I've been pouring over *The Bipolar Survival Guide: What you and your family need to know* (2011: J. Miklowitz, PhD). There in black and white are detailed descriptions of aspects of Neil's response to daily life that either hurt or annoyed me. I remember one night in 2009 when we were walking back to our hotel in Palm Springs after a late supper. The night was black and the road deserted. I limped along with the support of my Canadian crutch wrapped around my forearm. Neil started walking faster and finally snapped, "Meet you at the hotel." I was scared on that dark street but couldn't quicken my pace. The next night I insisted we take a lighted road with other people around.

How I wish I'd known then that the need to hurry, the feeling that other people are moving too slowly, is just one common phase of the bipolar mood swings. Had I found such books during my marriage, at least my feathers would have been less ruffled. I loved the title of Chapter One, "How This Book Can Help You Survive—and Thrive." On page after page, I found *aha* moments. I wished that Neil and I had had the benefit of advice like this and yet I also marvelled at the way we were helped by friends and even strangers.

WRITING THE UNITAS NEWSLETTER AND ORGANIZING MEDITATION CONFERENCES

I had been impressed by the courage with which Fr. Laurence, the young English-born successor of John Main, had faced the death of Fr. John and the resulting heavy burden of expectations that fell on his shoulders. He was barely thirty, with only a short time as a monk at Ealing before he came with Fr. John to Montreal. While Fr. John was alive, I had kept a certain distance from the monastery. We were invited to the oblate meetings, but neither of us made the formal vows. Now, we started to think about what to do to make good on our promise to Fr. John that we would keep something going. It seemed to me inappropriate for people like ourselves to wait for a much younger Fr. Laurence to show us what to do, when we could use our years of experience to figure it out ourselves.

In the late 1970s we had invited John and Clare Hallward to a Swiss fondue supper at the Alpenhaus and said, "You have to meet this man, John Main." They became involved and remained with the Pine Avenue group ever since. Now the four of us met in our living room to talk about starting a newsletter for the meditation network. We called the newsletter *UNITAS*. It proved to be a link for many far-flung groups, a forum where lay people in particular could find a voice, as we explored the implications of meditation in our everyday lives.

We pitched the idea to a focus group in another city. They were enthusiastic and said to me, "and you will be the editor. Your ecumenical background makes you the ideal person." I had assumed Neil would be the editor. He had worked for a year on the prestigious Jesuit magazine *America* in New York. Finally, I suggested that Clare Hallward and I take turns as editor of alternate issues, and the other would focus on looking for stories. Sharing the roles would be more fun for both of us. Ultimately we were a team of four whose skills were remarkably complementary. John, who had been editor of *The Isis* newspaper at Oxford, wrote key articles and did important interviews, as did Neil.

As we worked on the newsletter, I remembered Fr. John's words in September 1982, on the fifth anniversary of his arrival in Montreal. He had talked about a "fellowship of friends." There was a sense of urgency in his words. He said, "We have so little time together; we need to cherish each other." This rang true to me and I thought about it for many months.

Fr. Laurence was generous in his support, giving us a free hand and allocating the financial resources. We worked well together. Doreen Romandini had exceptional organizational skills and brought together a team of volunteers for the task of mailing ten thousand newsletters all over the world. It was a happy and productive time.

Best of all, this vehicle gave us a chance to meet and hear from some unusual people. One was a young Baptist minister who at the early age of 19 had worked in the Nova Scotia prisons with offenders of varying degrees, some of whom were locked away for life and who saw themselves as the outcasts of society. A Catholic nun had taught him to meditate and he formed a group among these men. One offender had blocked out the crime he had committed. He said to the young minister, "I am afraid of what God will say to me. Please hold my hand as I meditate." He had a dream that he was falling and falling toward the centre of the universe. A sign said, 'There is more for you.' He found himself at the centre of the universe. He was being held, and he was loved. He was able to remember the crime and begin working toward rehabilitation.

By the end of the 1980s, Fr. Laurence had moved to England and the last of the Benedictines had left the Pine Avenue meditation centre. After years of successfully publishing *UNITAS*, we decided to move on to other projects and leave the newsletter to Fr. Laurence and a new team working out of England.

When Fr. John died and we needed a strong vision of community, I knew what to do. There were people scattered in many different places who had learned to meditate as a result of Fr. John's work, many of whom we had never met. No one really knew how many small, isolated groups had formed, how to find them or whether they were still active. I remembered the Sixties slogan, "Think globally, act locally."

Over the next ten years, I organized three international conferences of meditation group leaders with the help of a dedicated group of oblates. I decided we needed to bring together people who were already familiar with the practice of meditation. Sister Gertrude McLaughlin was an enthusiastic supporter during many months of preparation. I thought twenty-five people might turn up for the first weekend retreat, but to my delight, fifty arrived at the Villa Marguerite. Hidden in the trees on the outskirts of Montreal, this retreat centre on the north shore of the Island of Montreal was a tranquil place to meditate.

When I organized that first international conference after Fr. John's death, I asked Neil to welcome the participants. I loved organizing the conference but still had no confidence in my ability to speak in public. He said, "No, you do it," and stood quietly by my side as I did just that. He in turn agreed to lead the plenary sessions. Once more, we were working as a team.

At the second conference, Neil again led the plenary sessions, at my request. To his surprise and mine, he did a great deal of talking instead of bringing out the other participants who had travelled a long way.

In planning the third conference in 1992, I was nervous about having Neil lead the sessions, but if I couldn't find any other role for him, I felt I would have had to exit from my own involvement. The end result was a catastrophe both for us and for others.

By the third conference, group leaders turned up from Australia, New Zealand, Singapore, the Philippines, Ireland, the U.S. and Great Britain. They were a colourful ecumenical mixture of clergy, religious and lay people who shared both their wisdom and their questions. Ruth Fowler from Australia became a special friend with whom I have kept in contact over the years. Sister Madeleine Simon decided to hold a conference the following year in Great Britain where there were over 200 groups.

In retrospect, I wondered if I should have cancelled the third international conference or, as I think now, handed it over to someone else. For some time, I had had the uneasy feeling that this was not the right space for Neil.

As the event drew closer, I looked forward to seeing old friends again. As usual, there was a lot of preparation to be done. To my dismay, on the opening day, I came down with a cold and had no choice but to sleep it off. This turned out to be quite fortunate for me. One of my friends, thinking he was being helpful, raised a question at the first session about leadership problems in the Montreal community. It was utterly inappropriate given the international attendance, but the damage was done. A man from another group muttered something and Neil exploded.

Friends came to see me, and in subdued tones told me what had happened. "If only he could have said what he said without anger," one friend said. Friends from other parts of the country who had come for that meditation conference did their best to comfort me.

That night, Neil took eight sleeping pills. It was the beginning of a two-year nightmare. Back at home, my brilliant husband began to spend most of the day on the couch in the living room, his head turned to the wall. He was never able to meditate again, nor would it have been wise. Meditation is not recommended for anyone who is suicidal.

Fortunately, our family doctor, Dr. Mark Roper, had referred Neil to Dr. Pablo Cervantes for help. Initially the referral had been to discuss Neil's difficulty sleeping and his reliance on sleeping pills. Cervantes, then head of the Mood Disorders Clinic at the Montreal General Hospital, was a man with an exceptional talent for listening and prescribing. Those visits gave me a glimmer of hope that my husband might be able to find some level of traction in dealing with his mood swings.

Even though he was being treated by the top professional in the field, there had been problems with Neil's medication. During a holiday in Florida, when we found ourselves in the middle of a hurricane, he went through red lights and stop signs and crashed the rental car into a tree. When I ordered him into the back seat and took over the wheel, he was furious.

Another time, during a visit with his nephews and their wives, he forgot part of his medications. On the way to the airport he wove the car in and out of the oncoming traffic, with his nephew in the car behind us nearly vomiting. When we stopped at a red light, his nephew pounded on Neil's window. "Do you want me to drive?" he begged. "No," said Neil firmly. Never in my life was I so glad to hand over a car when we finally arrived at the airport.

As I remember incidents such as these, I ask myself what elements in my life helped me survive those often hair-raising and puzzling years. If I were even five minutes late leaving to go for supper at the Hallwards', Neil would blow up. I never knew what minor incident might trigger an outburst.

As long as all that bipolar energy was absorbed in his radio work, or writing, or his television show, Neil was fine, if outer appearances could be believed. Yet it was clear to me that under the surface of the talented man that I loved, some form of destructive energy could break out at any moment.

Still, despite his unpredictability, our cleaning lady remembers him as always courteous and thoughtful, making her a cup of coffee in the morning when she arrived. His producer, Daniel Freedman, during his three-year television stint at CFCF Television, noticed that Neil showed the same respect for a make-up artist, stage hand or waitress as he showed for a professor or Prime Minister.

A shining public figure plagued with inner turmoil and mood swings

Although Daniel, like everyone else in Neil's world, had no idea that Neil was bipolar, his description is a classic. "You never knew what to expect from Neil. He could be funny, he could be demanding, he could be endearing and Lord knows, he could be exasperating, all in the same conversation." His younger colleagues, Joan Takefman and Wendy Helfenbaum, were known on more than one occasion to exclaim, "He's out of control!" when he insisted on having a guest they didn't approve of.

It was never clear to me whether Neil ever came to realize the implications of being bipolar. In later years he discussed the subject of depression, "the dark places," with his friend Harold Thuringer. Yet he never once used the term bipolar to Harold or me, nor did he mention it in his memoir *The Inside Story*, where he writes extensively about depression and its effects. It still puzzles me that Neil never used the term.

DEPRESSION STRIKES
1992 – 1994

During those weeks and months there was little verbal communication between Neil and me. I didn't even try to initiate any conversation. There were no words for what was going on. As he lay on the couch, hour after hour, all I knew to do was to tune in to his soul with all the energy in my being.

For two years Neil was on the brink of suicide. As he experienced the full force of bipolar depression, most of his day was spent on the long couch in our living room. On weekday afternoons, he would drag himself to his feet and take a taxi to CJAD, where he was part of an ongoing conversation. At supper he would sit silently watching the evening news on CNN. As the evening wore on, I could feel the room filling with dark energy, as though we were in the middle of *Star Wars*. There were two battles raging. Neil was in a single-handed combat with Darth Vader. My challenge was to not give into the darkness, but to try to break up the bad energy by heading straight for the heart of the Death Star, as Luke Skywalker did.

I did my best to keep life as normal as possible. After preparing meals and cleaning house, I walked to the meditation centre on Pine Avenue where I continued to volunteer. By late afternoon I was back home preparing supper. As the night closed in, my dread of the dark energy increased.

One night the energy was so terrifying I fled the house in a panic. I headed toward Victoria Village, two blocks of small boutiques and cozy coffee shops where one might run into a neighbour or two. At the corner of Somerville and Prince Albert, I saw a familiar figure. It was Joyce McNamara, walking her two small dogs. I rushed up to her and stopped her in her tracks, nearly tripping as the dog's leash wrapped around my legs. We stood talking and gradually my panic subsided as I grounded myself. After a few minutes, we said goodbye and I was able to return to the house in a calmer frame of mind. By the time I got home, the dark energy there had receded. But in the depths of my being I felt I had lost a marriage, a home and the husband I loved.

One evening, as I sat quietly in my chair by the fireplace, with Neil resting on the sofa, an image arose in my consciousness, as it had when I was an eight-year-old child. The two of us were surrounded by a cloud of love, separated from the next world only by a thin curtain. By then I was so physically and emotionally exhausted, I was losing a grip on this world and felt that I could almost blow away through the thin veil.

Two days later, I went to see the movie *Babette's Feast*, the story of a refugee from Marseille who lands up in a small village in Denmark where people have stopped talking to each other. She creates a magnificent feast that changes everything. At one point during the feast, a general gets up who had abandoned the village and the love of his life. As he stands there he says, "In the end, regardless of our choices, all that remains is the infinite love of God." I clung to that sentence to maintain my sanity.

That year we went for our usual summer visit to Madawaska Island in the St. Lawrence River. Neil told me later that plans were swirling in his head to end his life by drowning, making it look like an accident. I had no language to talk to anyone about what we were going through nor did anyone in my family. They knew something was terribly wrong but it was beyond everyone's realm of comfort to even try to talk about it. Until recently, this inability to speak about what was happening has been an unfortunate and even dangerous aspect of bipolar depression. It was a painful time for everyone.

Gradually, however, as autumn turned to winter, Neil began to feel much better. We were able to drive up to the Laurentians with our skis to Rivière du Diable in Parc Mont Tremblant. I remember standing in the sunshine laughing. The next morning, back in Montreal, Neil held me tight and said, "Catharine, I'm plunging down worse than ever. I'm terrified." I made him breakfast and then in a way I could neither explain nor justify, I left the house and went up to the meditation centre. I sat there shaking until four o'clock, until suddenly I knew he was alright. In his memoir, Neil describes what happened after I left.

> I had long since given up the idea of a gun or death by drowning. The tape now playing was about a plunge onto the tracks of the Montreal metro. I knew this would be messy for me and for those who survived me, especially Catharine. But I was no longer thinking of others. My inner being was like an inkwell, overflowing with black thoughts of nothing but myself.
>
> I pushed off the blanket and got up from the couch, my body heavy and laden. I watched my next movements as though I was a spectator in a dark cinema. Slowly and laboriously, I found a pencil and a piece of paper and wrote a one-sentence suicide

note: Dearest Catharine, I think you will be better off without me. Love, Neil. Then I folded the note, my own obituary notice, and placed it carefully on the floor just inside the front door.

It was a windy March day. I put on my parka, locked the front door and shuffled along to a bar on Sherbrooke Street. I thought it would be easier if I had a drink, although I had not had one in years. The world around me, the people, the cars, the stores with Easter decorations, seemed unreal as if I was looking into a green-coloured fish tank. I sat at the bar for a few minutes but didn't order a drink. Then I trudged to the Vendôme metro station, just west of my home in Westmount. I walked down the steps into the metro, went out onto the apron, and sat on a bench about twenty feet from the tracks. I stared glassily as about half a dozen trains roared by. Then I got up and went back home. I think I was then, for just a moment, in a moment of calm – the eye of the storm. The physical activity of walking in the fresh cold air had briefly stilled the suicide tapes and given me just enough momentum to take a tiny positive step. Back home, I dialed the telephone number of my young friend, Chris, with whom I had breakfast occasionally. I don't know what the outcome would have been had he not answered. But he did and invited me to join him for supper at a neighbourhood restaurant. I agreed, went to the front door and tore up the suicide note. The telephone rang. It was Catharine. I could hear the relief in her voice when I answered and when I told her I was having supper with Chris. Much later, she told me that about half an hour before, just when I was telephoning Chris, she somehow knew it was going to be alright.

While picking at supper, I described for Chris as well as I could what a hell hole I had been in all day. Then, with a kind of groan and a strangled voice that came from deep inside me, I said to him, "I just want to be real." Only six words, but they described and distilled a lifetime. I could no longer endure the split of feeling one way about myself but needing others to feel another way. I could no longer summon the energy to bear the mask to maintain that charade, no longer wanted to be a performer. I desperately wanted to be real and needed help to make the journey. Chris said he wanted me to go with him to meet a friend. Little did I realize this friend would guide me on a new journey and save my life.

The friend that Chris introduced Neil to was Jim, who became Neil's A.A. buddy and the older brother Neil never had. For my part, I would strongly urge any family member living with this form of mental illness to find a related self-help group or at least call the depression hot-line.

INSTITUTE FOR HUMAN GROWTH

At that time I was told about the Institute for Integral Human Growth, started by a physical education teacher who was given a group of seventeen- and eighteen-year-olds from a reformatory. She was told they were a lost cause. "That can't be true," she thought and started paying attention to the small things they did well. She noticed that those elements in their behaviour began to grow. She then studied psychology and ended up creating the Institut du Développement humain intégral, where the emphasis was on paying attention to your own strengths and those of other people.

Helen Kilimnik, a much respected nun, was the director when I attended in 1993. It was clear to me that she was unafraid of depression and all its implications. "Depressions usually last eighteen months," she told me. Up until then I had felt paralysed, helplessly watching my husband walk along the edge of a cliff. I was terrified to call out in case he fell off.

One day I was driving to the Institute when a young man drove right through a stop sign and crashed into my car. This young man had no insurance and was heartbroken to lose his car. I, on the other hand, was greatly relieved. It meant that Neil and I had to stop driving for a couple of weeks while the car was in the garage. Helen just looked at me when she heard this story.

AL-ANON

One night I had a dream. In it a friend said to me, "You are becoming ill and everyone can see it." I shot out of bed and that morning went to an A.A.-Al-Anon conference that I had happened to see advertised.

When Neil proposed marriage to me he was very honest about the fact that he was a recovering alcoholic with three years of sobriety behind him. No big deal, I thought at the time. My Uncle Lloyd was a recovering alcoholic who had won my heart as a child by blowing cigarette smoke rings out of his ears and treating me as though I mattered. I had often gone with Neil to 'open' A.A. meetings, notably in the early years of our marriage. I felt very comfortable at these meetings but never spoke to Neil about them.

Since Neil had gone to A.A. early in our marriage, I had ventured into Al-Anon, a group for people with alcoholic family members. But at the very first meeting in a local hall, I saw a close neighbour. I was speechless and embarrassed and never went back, feeling that I had betrayed Neil's public image.

Now, twenty years later, desperate for help, I slipped into the back row of a large Al-Anon plenary session. A doctor was speaking, emphasizing the point that we should never second guess ourselves about the way that we deal with alcoholism in the family. "It's a horrendous disease," he said. I agreed, but I had yet to realize that the underlying cause of what I was living through with Neil had less to do with alcoholism and more to do with the effects of bipolar disorder. Alcoholism was one way of self-medicating a depressive disorder.

As the A.A. meeting drew to a close, I spotted a woman whom I had seen at the Al-Anon meeting I had run out of twenty years earlier. Before I could change my mind, I rushed up to her and blurted out, "I need to talk." She ended up inviting me to the Thursday night group that she attended in the West Island. "I'll pick you up at five," she said. The die was cast. I was driven with three other women to a pleasant restaurant and to my amazement all we did for an hour was laugh our fool heads off, enjoying a good meal before going to the meeting.

For the first time I found a language to express what I was going through. I was with people who understood. One friend said, "We do the best we can, even if it isn't very good." What a relief.

I continued those Thursday outings much to Neil's annoyance. "Where are you going?" he barked each time I went out the front door. When I told him that I was going to Al-Anon, he would try to keep me at home.

Later he told me with considerable regret that in the depths of his despair he tried to pull me down with him. I knew, however, that I had to look after my own health, even though I was afraid to leave him alone in the house.

Amazingly, even during the dreadful time of his depression, Neil kept the *Exchange* discussions going at our home. It must have been a huge effort for him during those two years. I wasn't required to participate in the discussion, but for me it was an effort just to clean up from supper, prepare a small snack, greet our guests and stay awake through the evening. Somehow we both did it and I was grateful for the supportive presence of our friends.

Through all of this, I was determined to keep busy, spending as much time as possible at the Pine Avenue meditation centre. Dr. Cervantes continued to adjust Neil's medications and provide a relaxing atmosphere for a form of talking therapy. At one point, he and Neil discussed the possibility of shock treatment. Neil decided to try it. By this point, he was far beyond any embarrassment about needing this treatment. He was placed in the psychiatric ward of the Montreal General Hospital. I would walk from the hospital through the parking lot to the Pine Avenue meditation centre. As I walked, I found myself saying, "The Lord is my shepherd," over and over again. Those five words remain my walking mantra to this day. I say them whenever I am afraid or upset, or simply to maintain my balance.

I realize now that the experience of being alone so much as a child, combined with the profound faith of my mother and grandmother, gave me a basis for survival when I found myself in the greatest crisis of my life with my husband's depression.

Ultimately, the shock treatments did not work because the young nursing assistant had not noticed that Neil was still taking sleeping pills.

Nevertheless, as the days wore on, my own sense of hope deepened. Neil began to move about more, even though he appeared to have aged dramatically. One evening when we went out for supper with Clare and John Hallward, Clare noted with considerable grief that Neil was shuffling like an old man.

CREATING PINE AVENUE PROGRAMMING

After the Benedictines left, a small group of us decided we needed to "carry on something" at the house on Pine Avenue. We were given a mandate by the Catholic bishop to run the Centre and to create programming. We knew many people and now turned to them for wisdom. We invited six priests to take turns saying mass on Friday evenings. When one of them looked at the tiny group gathered around the altar in the huge room that once had been crammed with people, he sighed, "This is pathetic."

At our invitation, people started turning up to share their wisdom, including a Baptist scholar and a Buddhist monk in his saffron robes. Later we discovered he was the Dalai Lama's representative in Canada.

Someone at the Diocesan Book Room told me later that an Australian music therapist and meditator, Marie Benveniste, was looking for a place to share her skills. Soon the whole house was full of music and people. Every noon hour, Marie came for meditation and we were able to start a regular group.

Monday and Tuesday evenings Patricia Murphy, an overloaded teacher who taught teenagers all day, arrived at 7:15 to turn on the lights and set up the room for the evening's meditation. Some people sat on cushions, others on chairs. We were fewer than in the days of John Main, but we were a faithful group and occasionally new people joined us.

At times the house was dark and empty. Once I arrived in the whirling snow to prepare for an event. The wind had blown the framed programme off the hook beside the massive brass-knobbed front doors. Shattered glass lay all over the snowy steps, and a rat had expired in the cold.

I stepped over the dead rat and the glass, went through the darkened halls into the kitchen, and turned on the oven to prepare hot food for our guests. Normally this was done by the Benedictine monks but since the last had departed, the lay people were now in charge of the big house and all preparations for its activities.

I went upstairs to prepare a room for our first overnight guest, a lecturer from Ottawa who was to give a workshop on meditation. I climbed the stairs slowly as the second floor had always been the monks' quarters. I was shy to enter. Suddenly, an inner voice spoke to me, saying, "Come on, what are you waiting for?" I felt myself swept along by a field of energy all around me.

Patricia Murphy was one of the early members of John Main's Montreal community. She had a special way of asking people to give a talk so that they couldn't say no. She succeeded in enlisting fifty people to give presentations, many of whom had never spoken before a group. Eight or nine people who had been meditating regularly took turns addressing the group. David Roffey, a Benedictine oblate and an artist, gave most of the Monday night introductory talks.

It was an extraordinary experience to find ourselves sitting in the chair once occupied by Fr. John. He had said, "One beggar showing the other where the bread is; meditation is caught, not taught." What was important was that we meditate together. Meditation was an experience beyond words, yet we had to find a way to talk about it. It was fascinating to see each person find his or her own voice.

I began by reading and rereading what Fr. John had written. As I imagined his voice speaking these words, images began surfacing. I found myself in the desert with the people of Israel, led by a pillar of fire through the darkness. That pillar of fire goes ahead of us, even though we can't see it. That image remains with me as a symbol of this time. Phrases from the psalms and stories that I had been told from my youth at Donlands began resurfacing.

I began to see my own life story inserted in the great sweep of the Jewish and Christian scriptures. Fr. John had quoted St. Paul in a way that made it seem as though we were hearing those insights for the first time.

For the lay people at the Pine Avenue house, the experience of having to give talks made us doubly appreciative of the training and skills of clergy and nuns. I marvelled at the wisdom shared by each one who presented to the group, many for the first time in their lives. I had written speeches for others, but was terrified to give a talk myself. Neil said that my first talk was like a string of clothes on a clothesline, with no connection between the thoughts. Some months later, he told me that my recent talk was the best he had ever heard, and it was all my own. Whether my presentations were the best or resembled a clothesline, even if no one else benefitted from my efforts, I certainly did.

TAIZÉ

One day, a group of seven young people asked if they could use the house for a weekend. They wanted to share what they experienced at a great Taizé gathering in Dayton, Ohio, organized by the American Catholic bishops. Taizé was started by a group of monks in France who had worked with the poorest of the poor. The lay monks also wrote songs. To their surprise, throngs of young people showed up to share in the songs. To accommodate the interest, the monks built a separate building for them, and even then, scores of tents were set up in the fields at certain times of the year.

As these seven toured the house, it was as if the whole place lit up to welcome them. One young man, with his ponytail braided neatly and the knees cut of out his jeans, said, "This house just wraps you around." When we came to the door of Father John's study, I knew that former headmaster would have welcomed these new arrivals.

In preparation for the weekend, six of us volunteers came after our daytime jobs ended at five o'clock to prepare the house. We opened up a whole wing of the house that had been shut down to save heat. Toilets were scrubbed and wooden floors polished. The Friday of that weekend, Montreal was struck by a huge snow storm. The truck with the food got stuck in the long driveway. A dozen organizers formed a chain and hoisted the food to the kitchen for a hot meal for fifty young people. Sleeping bags appeared in unlikely corners.

The whole weekend was a powerful experience of Spirit. The Taizé music alternated with a silence so deep you could almost touch it. "You can feel the prayer in these walls," one young woman said. With tears streaming down her cheeks, she talked of the dryness in her life.

During the night, I went around occasionally to see if a pipe had burst. A conversation on the landing continued until five in the morning. It was led by a young pastoral animator, Peter Vaillancourt. I was surprised at its sustained depth, but shouldn't have been. He had already led one group up in a tree in Hudson, Quebec. A policeman stopped by and said, "What on earth are you doing?" "Praying," they answered. The policeman climbed up and joined them.

A year later, Peter led another Taizé group at the house. Seventy young people turned up. Alone in the house after the young people had left, a line by T.S. Eliot rang through my mind. He concluded the poem *Little Gidding* with the line, "And the fire and the rose are one."

Soon afterward at the meditation centre, I was sitting in an armchair by the fire in what been the McConnell family dining room before the house had been given to Fr. John. I was very tired. I sat lulled by the fire and wondered idly when T.S. Eliot's rose would show up. The next day, the back doorbell rang. A volunteer, Hugette Marcoux, answered it and came back carrying a huge rosebush full of yellow roses. It was a gift for the house from a grower she had met.

Jim and Neil at the Barack Obama – Hillary Clinton debate in 2008

In the spring, knowing that Neil was recovering well after his depression, thanks to his own efforts and the support of his A.A. friend Jim, I travelled to France to spend a week at Taizé. I wanted to discover for myself what lay behind the spirit of those weekends. I arrived at the Taizé Community at Saône-et-Loire in Burgundy in a heat-wave at the end of April. Abruptly, a sleet storm came roaring in from the Swiss Alps and the whole place turned to mud. I opened my window the next morning, and there on a branch in front of me, a single rose had bloomed. I walked over to the main building and saw a tiny fire. No one else was there. I warmed myself for a few minutes before a young woman came in. She gave me a broken broom handle, the finest staff I'd ever seen. This is exactly what I needed to be able to walk steadily in the mud.

The brothers at Taizé spoke of doing a little with love, of a God who doesn't ask more of us than we can give. Aunt Polly, whose love enriched so many people from behind the counter of her tiny grocery store, would have agreed.

Pen to Paper 1998 – 2012

Montreal Ice Storm

In January 1998, I booked myself into the Villa Marguerite for a peaceful two-week period of writing. One evening I was writing in my room when I heard an ominous crack of thunder that seemed almost overhead. I looked out the window at the nearby bridge over the river. A truck was making its way slowly onto the Island of Montreal. As it travelled, the lights on the bridge went out, one by one. By now, the wind was howling, accompanied by a puzzling sound, louder than rain. We were beginning the storm to end the millennium, the Montreal Ice Storm—days of raining ice that virtually paralyzed the island of Montreal as thousands of homes lost power and heat. The entire island turned into a sheet of ice and travel became treacherous.

Fortunately, the retreat house had a generator. The next morning I was making my way down to the dining room for breakfast, when I found myself surrounded by wheelchairs and the hallways buzzing with many voices. A nearby seniors' home with no generator had evacuated its dozens of residents into the Villa Marguerite.

For the next few days, every time I left my room, I had to navigate walkers and wheelchairs, with cheery voices commenting on my progress. The original eighty-seven pages of this manuscript were written during that storm.

Meanwhile, Neil was at home alone. Fortunately I didn't know what he was up to, but when the Canadian army arrived, he immediately went to see what they were doing, with ice-burdened trees falling in all directions. Our house had no power, but we had some food provisions in our root cellar. For the first couple of days, he survived with breakfast at Murray's Restaurant.

Then Clare Hallward received a phone call from Neil. "I'm sitting here in the dark, Clare, what shall I do?" "Neil, do you have a flashlight?" she asked. "Well, yes," he said, "but I don't know where Catharine put it." Clare knew that there were always candles on our dining room table for the evening meal. "Neil, do you know where the matches are?" "No." "Well, Neil, I think you had better come and stay with us," she said finally. Of course that's just what Neil was hoping to hear.

FROM MY WRITINGS DURING THE 1998 ICE STORM

An article appeared in *L'Actualité* exploring the effects Montreal's two main cultures had had on each other. In the views of the writers, most of them had been a benefit, giving birth to a new society. Montreal still seems to me to possess a very special dynamic. This is showing itself as I write. Outside the retreat house, the wind is howling, bringing temperatures below 30 degrees below zero. Eight days ago, the day I came here, in January 1998, the worst ice-storm in Canada's history hit with full force. Three million people have been without power. Soldiers coming in to the area had the impression of coming into a war zone, with transmitters crumpled like matchsticks, and thousands of people in shelters. Friends have been on the phone from Europe and the U.S. concerned about the pictures they have seen on the nightly news. Families without food and heat have arrived here at the Villa Marguerite along with a husky puppy, babies, children and a parakeet. People talk of being helped by strangers.

The French T.V. station sent out a call for volunteers. An hour later a busload headed out to one of the shelters, full of volunteers, food and clothing. Huge truckloads of wood, beds and other necessities came in from the Saguenay where people had experienced the generosity of the whole country just a year ago.

In times like this, Quebecers go way beyond politics as I have seen them do time and again. Because of La Relance, I've been involved with a whole network of people from the East End, Les Canadiens hockey team, employees of IBM, and individuals from the West End to provide some food and services for some of the poorest families in the city.

DREAM SISTERS

I held onto Peribonka until it became financially impossible. When I regretfully sold the cottage in 1998, I used the proceeds from the sale to create the Fleming McKenty Foundation to assist a variety of community projects. It was the only thing I could do with the home that had given me more than sixty years of happy memories. It had been Granny Fleming's wedding gift to my parents. My dad was there all too briefly. A photo of the screen front door shows an almost invisible person about to step out. I liked to think that it was my dad.

On the last evening, I sat with Neil in front of the big stone fireplace in the living room until the last log had burned. Then I stayed up most of the night watching the flickering patterns of the Northern Lights dance over the lake. The next morning I struggled out of bed, folded up the blanket and sheets and got dressed. Then I went out on the balcony off my room to have one last look at the lake.

There, swimming serenely near the shore, not far from the spot where little fishes used to nibble my toes, was a mother duck with six small ducklings bobbing along behind her. "She's come to say goodbye to me," I thought. With a smile and a wave, I closed the door to the balcony, locked it and went downstairs to prepare one last breakfast. We ate our meal in the kitchen at the old wooden table, then washed up.

Neil lifted our packed bags into the car while I locked the front and kitchen doors for the last time. He got behind the wheel, then drove us slowly along the lane. I didn't look back but kept my gaze steadily on the dirt road ahead of us. As we were about to pass under the spreading branches of two vast oak trees, I looked up. Gazing serenely at us were two large ospreys. I had never seen such huge birds at Peribonka. As they perched there, the sunlight shone down around them. Their gaze was a final blessing before we set out on the seven-hour drive back to Montreal.

By the time we reached Somerville Avenue, I was exhausted. That first night home, I fell into a profound sleep. A vivid dream took over my whole being. Four young women in white dresses were diving into the waters of Lake Simcoe right in front of Peribonka.

I knew with complete certainty who three of the young women were. There was Laurie, a bright young lawyer now living in the U.S. There was Sona, whom I had visited at her home in England. There was Tara Lee, involved in community work near Quebec City. But who was the fourth? I had no idea. I thought, "Perhaps I'd better go looking for her." I pondered the dream but there was nothing more I could do, so gradually it receded.

Laurie was a talented law student when Neil and I met her. She graduated from McGill Law School, then left Montreal to work as a volunteer in France with L'Arche, an international foundation dedicated to improving the lives of people with intellectual disabilities. Back in the U.S., she worked as a child advocate. Then we heard that she had had a life threatening operation to remove a neuroendocrine tumour on her spine and was recuperating at her home in New Hampshire.

Later, there was a recurrence of the tumour and this time it was inoperable. Laurie's spirit amazed me. Each time I talked to her, she was upbeat, open about the reality she was living but focussed on life itself.

Most recently she told me, "I am seeing my more obvious symptoms as a kind of new gift." We had a good laugh about the way the Parisians at L'Arche had dealt with her Montreal 'franglais', as we call the combination of English and French in Quebec. "We've got to clean her up," they said. And by the end of the year, her French was pretty good. Loving language as she does, it is hard for Laurie to find her own speech slowing down. I am very proud of her and grateful that she is in my life.

I met Sona, my second dream daughter, when she came to Montreal as a volunteer at the Pine Avenue meditation centre. She had just spent a year at Taizé, in France, and would be in Montreal for four months. Her father was Indian and her mother English, a rich heritage.

The months in Montreal were difficult for her, as she had invested in a romance that didn't work out. She wisely went off on a trip to India to gain a fresh perspective. Then she returned to England, where she had grown up and could reconnect with her parents.

In no time a romance was brewing again, this time a very solid one. Marriage and a new career followed. Sona and her husband, James, had two children and settled in England. While homeschooling their daughters, they worked for the development of the National Shrine to Our Lady in the small village of Walsingham, Norfolk, on the East coast of England. In medieval times it was one of the four major pilgrimage shrines in Christendom along with Jerusalem, Rome and Santiago.

Sona and James had been married seven years when I arrived in England. Their very lively five-year-old girl, Sophia, thrust a beautifully illustrated picture book into my hands and asked me to read to her. Did you know that aliens like to steal human underwear? Well, neither did I. As I read out loud, I discovered that aliens might wear our underwear on their hands, on their feet or even on their heads. The young lady then climbed out of the window, leaving me to rush to call her mother, who was unflappable.

I had met the third dream daughter, Tara Lee, some years before when she was still a student. Neil and I helped her with school fees and such. She wrote:

> I live in a small village outside of Quebec City called Stoneham and am blessed with two beautiful children, Charlotte 4 and Liam 6, and a loving husband. I continue to work as a Consultant for our English School Board and my husband works part time in order to be a stay at home dad.

Although getting to work can be quite the commute at times, the fresh air and connection with nature does wonders for our souls. Seeing the world through the eyes of our children is a true blessing. Their innocence and pure spirit are gentle reminders of our need for laughter and playfulness in our otherwise busy and hectic work life. Liam started skiing and feels he has found his true calling in life while Charlotte feels she can dance her way to stardom...they keep us young in spirit.

My days of visiting 66 Somerville Avenue, sharing a meal and great conversation are fond memories I will always cherish for they were instrumental in why I have found happiness today. To my dream sisters, through Catharine's love we have found each other... I hope to one day meet together to share our stories...

The days following the sale of Peribonka were busy ones. Neil was supportive of my decision to turn the proceeds of the sale of Peribonka into a charitable foundation. It was clear we would make decisions together, for which I was grateful. One of the first recipients of a grant was Dans La Rue.

Neil learned that the founder of Dans La Rue, Father Emmett Johns, known to Montrealers as Pops, had a booth at an upcoming event. Pops founded Dans La Rue in 1988, purchasing a mobile camper to serve hot food to homeless youth in Montreal. That afternoon we arrived at the hotel downtown and saw Pops sitting quietly at his place. There was a young woman in her twenties at the booth, talking animatedly with people. I watched her for a few minutes, then approached her and we started talking. "Would you like to join me for a cup of tea?" I asked. I followed that with an invitation to lunch at Beauty's. Over lunch it hit me with complete certainty: *she's the fourth.* It had taken me only a few months to find her. That was more than twenty years ago.

Stéphanie had been thrown out of her home by an alcoholic mother when she was only fourteen, suddenly living on the street with only a garbage bag of her possessions and no money. She stayed briefly with the Director of Youth Protection but ran away often. Then she survived as best as she could, taking drugs, though not as heavily as some, living in an empty warehouse with other street kids, hoping no one would find them. It was during those years of sheer survival that she met Pops. He helped her get an apartment and go back to school, though she was reluctant at first. Neil and I were able to help her continue, finish high school, then go on to art school where she thrived.

Once Pops had gotten her off the street, she began going into schools with him, encouraging kids to stay off drugs. Having learned that nothing comes easily, she held down demanding jobs at the University of Montreal while completing her diploma. She met Jean Plourde, who had a stable job in maintenance at the University of Montreal. Jean told me that meeting Stéphanie and her daughter Léa changed his life and gave it meaning. They have been together for more than twenty years and have a son, Olivier, a daughter Léa, and a grandson, Louka. I hope Stéphanie enjoys reading this as much as I enjoyed writing it.

I always speak in superlatives about Stéphanie. When Neil and I sold the house on Somerville and moved into the seniors' residence, she organised everything and has been doing that ever since. When Neil died, she was right by my side. She began typing my memoir and did enormous work for me. At every stage since, she has helped me organize my papers and stuff. I still ask myself, "Who sent me that dream?"

Jean Plourde helped Neil solve various computer problems. Jean often sat cross-legged on the floor, totally absorbed in the task and the conversation. Neil himself had sat on the floor like that with students in Montreal. Jean once said to me, "It's amazing how two people like Neil and me who come from very different backgrounds—French/English, young man/someone his age—could come together and have discussions and debates about any and every subject.

"When I met Neil I didn't make the connection with the man I saw on his TV show but a few months after that I realized that he was the face I used to see in my living room when I was a young teenager. I didn't recognize him because he had grown a beard. One day Neil said, 'I have a blog.' I was so impressed that he continued to reach people with his great pen. Il continue de toucher les gens avec sa belle plume."

Stéphanie writes:

I always say that the year I met Catharine was my lucky year. The timing in my life was just perfect.

I was doing lots of talks and different events with Pops, from Dans La Rue. I was not that long ago a homeless youth who went to the van to have at least one meal a day, hot-dogs. Now, he was bringing me with him to talk to other kids and professionals about my experience. He didn't talk much, me on the other hand, had a lot to say.

I already had my daughter and I was trying to finish school. So here I was, in a hotel, downtown Montreal, in an event where the organisation Dans La Rue had a booth with Pops explaining to a group of people what the organisation did for the homeless youth. In the back of the group I could see a tall, blonde, older woman with a magnificent hat on her head covered with flowers. Fast in my mind, as I was talking I was drawn to her.

After I finished and people went, I was preparing the booth and getting ready for a new talk when she approached me. I cannot describe what went through my mind. It was as if we were just meant to meet. She said:

- Hi! My name is Catharine McKenty, would you like to have a cup a tea with me sometime?

- Yes! Why not? I replied instantly.

I have to put this in context a little. I was not as social as a 23-year-old doing talks in school may be. My trust in people was almost non-existent. But something in me knew that Catharine was a special person. So I jumped at the opportunity to have a new friend.

After our first get together at Beauty's I couldn't believe that someone like her was interested in me, in what I had to say. I could see in her eyes that she was listening and engaged in what I was telling her. It was almost surrealist for me. I think I talked a lot and she listened for our couple of next meetings. Every time I was going back home I felt stronger and less alone.

I did learn so many things about myself, my life, my mother, about relationships, about so much. She was always my first person to go to if I needed advice and a hug. I would never be the woman I am today without her. Surprisingly, I didn't hear about the dream, I think, until ten years later. I met with Sona and Tara Lee but I am in contact every week with Laurie. And between each other we all call ourselves Dream Sisters.

I see Catharine every week, and try to be as present as I can. We are meant to be in each other's life, we have lots of fun and interesting conversations, projects and laughter.

Recently, Stéphanie started working at the Superior Court of Quebec. As Court Clerk, she organizes jury duty at times, introduces the judges to the court, or travels seventeen floors delivering mail. I was not surprised to be told that the judges and other personnel are pleased with her work. Eventually this will lead to a full-time job. It means of course that she is able to spend less time with me, but we are regularly in touch.

At Christmas-time, Stéphanie, Léa and Louka came for dinner. What a joy! Louka, now four months old, stole everyone's heart. He is a happy baby. At the time of my 88th birthday, the four dream daughters presented me with the cutest tiny toy dog. I call her Dreamy.

A new friend, Jeri Pitzel, has come aboard for the production of this book. She works in the corporate world, preparing corporate bids

Catharine in 1998, wearing the hat that dream daughter Stephanie described as magnificent

from content submitted by five or ten colleagues. She therefore copes effortlessly with the challenges of combining my scores of separate stories into a single main text. What a relief!

Writing Weekends 1996-1998

At one point, John and Clare Hallward, my cousins Bob and Patsy Fleming, and Neil and I talked about the interest we each had in reading other's work as well as writing for fun and in our chosen professions.

"What about getting together for a writing weekend?" Neil suggested. "There is a lovely resort north of Kingston where we could stay and have an enjoyable time." That was the start of an experience that proved to be richer than any of us could have foreseen.

My cousin Bob wrote a piece about his father, Lloyd Fleming, which helped him to heal his painful memories. Uncle Lloyd's battle with alcoholism came close to destroying his relationship with his sons and grandchildren. Then he made that crucial phone call to A.A. What was truly amazing was that out of all that suffering, Uncle Lloyd became the founder of A.A. in Spain, beginning in the south of the country in the Malaga area. My mother loved her older brother dearly. She remembered him playing Handel's Largo on the piano when they were growing up.

During the four years I was a young volunteer in Europe, Mum drove us down through France to the south of Spain three times to visit Uncle Lloyd. In the north, we passed through nearly deserted countryside, still showing signs of the devastation from the Civil War.

During the first of the visits, Uncle Lloyd sent us off in his Rolls Royce, driven by his chauffeur Paco, to see the Alhambra. There were no tourists at that time. I was blown away by the beauty of the Moorish architecture, a spiritual experience to treasure. My uncle also sent us to the shop of a young jeweller whose life had almost been destroyed by alcoholism. Mum bought me a bracelet he had fashioned, his life now on track, thanks to A.A.

Those writing weekends encouraged me to keep on scribbling.

WRITING THE LAURENTIAN LODGE SKI CLUB BOOK

At one point, I was asked to update the history of the Laurentian Lodge Ski Club near the town of Shawbridge that had been compiled by Alan Turner-Bone. I made some brief changes, added dates and so on, but I wasn't satisfied. There was something missing. I called Barbara Kemp who had been an early member of the club and asked her a few questions.

Barbara told me a story. She and a friend decided to climb on their skis up Mt. St-Hilaire, then spend the night three-quarters of

Neil at the Laurentian Lodge Ski Club, after one of Chef André's delicious meals

the way up at the ranger's lodge. When they got to their destination, they found the building full of male college students. No problem. They cut branches from nearby fir trees, made beds on top of the deep snow, and went happily to sleep.

In the middle of the night, they were awakened by a rustling sound. There were six pairs of eyes looking at them in the pitch black night. A pack of wolves was circling around them.

Fortunately, just at that moment, the door of the hut opened and one of the students came out for a smoke. Barbara and her friend scrambled for safety. It was only years later, Barbara told me, that she realized that those wolves were just curious.

It occurred to me that other older members of the club might have stories to tell. The manager, John Schwab, was able to find some lists of members from the early days of the Club, hidden away in the back of a filing cabinet. Quite a few of them were from outside of Quebec. A good number of Americans had come to the Club in the Thirties.

There was the phone number of Cleveland Dodge in New York. Talking to him, I learned that he was now seventy-eight. He had a vivid memory of coming to the Club with his parents when he was eight years old, in 1930, to visit Wilder Penfield and his wife in Montreal. Penfield, a neurosurgeon, was the founder of the Montreal Neurological Institute and an early member of the Club.

I sat furiously taking notes, as Clee Dodge told me a story that has gone down in Laurentian history.

> One day about the middle of February, we were out skiing near the Big Hill. I noticed two or three men who were mounting an auto chassis on large beams. They had mounted a pulley in place of one of the rear wheels. A rope was wound with several turns around the pulley. This rope was then extended up a small hill which was just north of the Big Hill. Curious to know what was going on, I skied over to the auto chassis. At that moment, the rope started to move slowly above the ground. I pointed my skis toward the hill and grabbed the rope with my gloved hands. The rope pulled me along the flat area in front of the hill. I was only eight years old and I found the rope

very heavy as I started moving up the hill, so I let go and fell away from the rope.

I did not visit the Shawbridge Club the winter of 1931. In January 1932, I returned with my parents. We found that the ski tow had been removed from the smaller north hill and was how located on the Big Hill.

It would seem the 1930 prototype, on which I rode, demonstrated that rope tows would work....Although it was a long time ago, I often told my family that I was the first person in the world to ride a ski tow, and indeed, I think I was.

The cumbersome contraption that had been rigged upon the Big Hill was soon known as "Foster's Folly," partly because at five cents a ride, or twenty-five cents a day, it never broke even. But it is recognized as the first ski tow in the world, a development that caused a revolution in skiing in North America, then in Europe.

As I talked to person after person who had ridden on that tow in their early years, it became clear it could be either hazardous or hilarious to use that tow. The pulley at the top could shred your mittens in a second, dropping them at your feet like shredded wheat. You could risk losing a hand or being choked to death by the rope. Or you might collapse, laughing, knocking down everyone behind you.

Another club member, Sally Drummond, helped me immeasurably in collecting all the stories. Sometime later, I showed three hundred pages to Neil. He said, "This is the best source material I have ever seen." He came on board, wove the stories into a clear pattern, wrote a lively introduction, and found a publisher, the inimitable Michael Price, founder of Price-Patterson.

Meanwhile, I scoured seven different archives for information and photos, including a clear photo portrait of Curé Antoine Labelle, one of the legendary figures in the history of the Laurentians. Known as the "roi du nord," Curé Labelle was over six feet tall and weighed 300 pounds. He was able to persuade Montrealers to fund the first stage of "Le Petit Train du Nord" as far as St. Jerome, opening the area to people from all over the continent, thus alleviating the extreme poverty of the farmers. Neil brought his story to life with vivid prose after I supplied him with the historical details. We worked well as a team. Having come through the darkness of the two-year depression, the experience was an incredible gift.

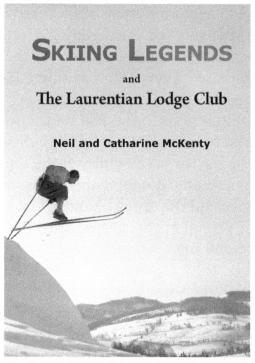

Cover of the book designed by Ted Sancton

Working on the ski book with Neil was like being in a graceful free-style ice dance routine. Our skills were complementary. I toured the archives and got in touch with early members of the Laurentian Lodge. Neil put everything together in a cohesive form.

Gone was the insistence on having supper in silence at six o'clock. Our dining room table was piled high with books about the formation of the Laurentian Mountains and the early history of skiing in Montreal and around Quebec, so we ended up going out for relaxed suppers across the road at the

Toucheh Restaurant. We were content to savour the food and the day's discoveries. Our publisher combined a stylish cover with easy to read print.

I filled up the trunk of our car with copies and together we tootled around to all the Montreal book stores. Our neighbours, Gerard and Gail Fellerath, did a book launch. To our delight, when we opened the *Montreal Gazette* one morning, there was *Skiing Legends and the Laurentian Lodge Club* on the bestseller list.

NEIL WRITES A MURDER MYSTERY

One of the biggest kafuffles during Neil's radio career occurred when Conservative Prime Minister Brian Mulroney agreed to go on the show but refused to take any calls. Why should he have to cope with any of those hostile Liberal listeners?

A staffer leaked the story to the *Montreal Gazette*, as Mulroney discovered when he was being driven in his limousine to the station. Neil was called into the management's office where a furious Mulroney was holding forth. He was, however, an astute politician, so he reluctantly agreed to go on the show and speak with callers. To his surprise, most of them were anything but hostile.

Much later I was sitting at the edge of the dance floor during a St. Patrick's ball that Neil and I always enjoyed. Mulroney and Brian Gallery walked by me on their way out the door. I heard Mulroney mutter to Brian, "McKenty certainly has mellowed." He was less complimentary when he discovered Neil had chosen *his street* for the setting of his murder mystery that was later published.

For this novel, Neil needed to envision an elegant house as the setting of the murder. He knew that Forden Avenue was the site of a lot of high-priced homes, including Mulroney's. So one day we drove up and down the street looking for a number that didn't exist, as the location for the murder of a socialite. When *The Other Key* was published in 2003, Mulroney was heard to moan, "Why did he have to do that?"

WRITING POLLY OF BRIDGEWATER FARM

From 2002-2009 I worked on the story of my own family. During my five visits to Ireland in those years, I became fascinated by Irish history. The resulting book centres around the life of my grandfather's older sister, Polly Noble, who left Ireland when she was ten years old. On January 6, 1839, the legendary Big Wind destroyed villages across Ireland, set thatched roofs on fire, and blinded children with cinders. It lifted hay ricks and corn stacks miles away, wrecked forty-two ships and toppled five hundred chimneys in Dublin. Across Ireland the Big Wind screamed like a thousand banshees as gusts blew to over 185 km/hour. Men and women ran half-naked into the streets, thinking the end of the world had come. Polly remembered her mother frantically dousing the wooden embers from the fireplace as they blew into the living room. As the wind howled, Polly, her older sister Eliza, and their widowed mother huddled, shivered and prayed. The small family emerged unharmed.

Two years later, Polly's widowed mother, Jane Caldwell Noble, married William Fleming, the handsome widower, age 33, from across the road. Polly was just four years old and her step-father's farm, Bridgewater Farm, became an enchanted place for her.

A year after their marriage, in 1842, her mother gave birth to a boy, Joseph Fleming. Joseph would later become a pioneering farmer in Manitoba, Western Canada, and founder of a large family network.

On November 8, 1844, Tyrone's first newspaper, the Tyrone Constitution, was founded by John Nelis, an Omagh printer and entrepreneur. That same year, the Globe was founded in Toronto by George Brown, its outspoken editor. He later teamed up with Irish-born Darcy McGee and Kingston lawyer John A. McDonald in the struggle to establish Canadian confederation, a broad and inclusive vision.

That same year Polly's mother, Jane Fleming, gave birth to twin girls. Polly's baby sisters, Isabella and Rebecca, became her special charge. Polly was only seven years old. The family continued to grow as hard times were mounting in Ireland. Years later, in Canada, Isabella became the mother of Joseph Thompson, Speaker of the Ontario Legislature; Rebecca's son was author/journalist Vern McAree.

In August 29, 1845, less than a year after its founding, the *Tyrone Constitution* newspaper (known as *"The Con"*) announced that "a fatal malady has affected the potato crop." By November, everyone knew that half of the potato crop had been lost. Forty-five percent of Irish farmers rented less than five acres and depended on this crop for survival. *The Con* noted that the oat crop alone could feed twice the population. Yet 16,000 quarters of oats were shipped each week out of the country to pay the exorbitant farm rents and taxes. This maintained the sanctity of a rigid economic policy imposed by politicians in distant London. In the midst of all this, William and Jane Fleming had a second son, bringing the number of children to seven: Eliza, Polly, Joseph, Rebecca, Isabelle, Maggie and Robert. As the situation in Ireland worsened, William's three brothers emigrated to Canada.

Ireland, winter 1846 – 1847. This winter was one of the coldest in living memory. In some areas it snowed for two months without stopping, cutting off food supplies for an already starving population. Roads were blocked, the potato crop was a total loss, typhus spread, and a million people died of fever and starvation. Jane and William Fleming, like more than one million others, decided to leave Ireland. Conditions on the island were appalling in spite of the efforts of many dedicated nurses, doctors and clergy, some of whom also died. The eighth child, Jane, was born just before they emigrated to Canada. In May 1847, William, Jane and their eight children travelled to Londonderry/Derry by cart and the first small train to ever run in that area.

On May 14, 1847, the Sesostris sailed for Quebec with 428 people on board a 600-tonne ship, with Captain Dand at the helm. They had just heard that seven Caldwells from Jane's Fermanagh clan were among the 411 passengers drowned when the ship Exmouth went down in a terrible storm. Jane, Polly's mother, realized that if her husband had not lost their fare at a game of cards, they, too, would have been on the Exmouth. Polly Noble Fleming, the second oldest of Jane and William's eight children, was a wide-eyed ten-year-old on a crowded ship at sea.

On June 14, 1847, the Sesostris arrived at Grosse Île, Quebec, only to find forty other sailing ships waiting to land at the quarantine station. During that stormy trip across the Atlantic, when they were housed under the deck, little Maggie, Robert, and the baby Jane all died and were buried at sea. At Grosse Île, Polly's beloved older sister Eliza died of fever and was buried in a mass grave. Polly became the oldest of the four surviving children.

The Fleming family stayed near relatives in Montreal, congregating with many other Irish in a province where French was the dominant language. After three years of struggling to eke out a small existence, they boarded the train for English-speaking Toronto.

On November 23, 1854, Jane gave birth to Robert Fleming, my grandfather, who was named after his brother who had died at sea. He was born on St. David Street; nearby Avenue Road and Bloor Street were two dusty trails. The horse ferry to Toronto Island was still running and the son of the owner of the Tecumseh Wigwam Tavern at the corner of Avenue Road and Bloor (later the site of the Park Plaza Hotel) was hanged for holding up a stage coach. A year later Jenny Lind, a notable local talent, was singing her heart out at the new meeting hall downtown, St. Lawrence Hall. Every ten minutes a horse-drawn omnibus took six people all the way from the new Hall up to the village of Yorkville, near the Bloor Street toll-gate. Barely a hundred gas lights lit up the town.

Polly's youngest brother Robert, or R.J., left the Park School at the age of twelve to take a job as an office boy and furnace stoker with T.W. Elliott, Flour and Feed, 53 George Street, Toronto, with whom he later became a partner. A dollar a day was good pay in those days, while young Robert worked for two dollars a week. In the streets of Cabbagetown, he gained a reputation as a scrapper who could beat up any kid on the block.

On May 15, 1854, when Polly was 17, she married John Verner in her parents' home on St. David Street. John had fought at the famous Battle of Ridgeway with the Queen's Own Rifles during the Fenian Raid of 1866. John was a promising tailor who made sure Polly always had a lovely dress to wear on special occasions. The marriage was performed by the Rev. Henry Wilkerson, then pastor of the old Richmond Street Methodist Church of which both were members. Afterward they lived on Victoria Street and then on James Street.

When John lost his well-paying job at the Custom House, he and Polly decided to open a grocery store. They built their home in the back of it on an empty lot on Parliament Street, just north of St. David Street where her parents lived.

They built their house in stages, including an outdoor privy and a stable. John and Polly had no children of their own, but they soon became parents to seven nieces and nephews who landed on their doorstep in need of a home. Soon, there were twelve and sometimes fifteen people living in a house built for six. After the death of their mother Jane in 1872, R.J., the neighbourhood scrapper, went to live with his sister Polly and her husband John. Under Polly's gentle but firm guidance, all that energy eventually went into politics. He went on to become two-time mayor of Toronto. After all the children in their care had left home, Polly and John joined the Metropolitan Church where Polly led a Sunday School class for many years.

I inherited a family bible dated 1890 from my aunt who had been a surgeon in India. It falls open at a story that was first told in our family by "Aunt Polly," as she is known to all of us. It was the story of a widow in the midst of a great famine. She had just enough oil and meal left to make a tiny cake for herself and her son before they starved. She went out of the village gates to gather a bit of firewood. She saw a man coming toward her, the prophet Elijah. He asked her to give him a little to eat, as the Lord had told him to do. To her it was an outrageous request. At first, she refused, then relented. From then on, the oil and the meal never ran out, and the village was fed. That story was at the heart of my own family. My mother told and retold it. During her lifetime, my mother gave away half of everything she owned.

Polly kept the whole family and many neighbouring families going with the help of that small grocery store. Throughout those years, the story of the prophet Elijah and the widow was told and retold. The grocery store was small and plain, a barrel of oysters sitting out front at Christmas time. Credit was offered to working class families, something the bigger stores did not do. Many of their customers worked at the Gas Company at the foot of Parliament Street, only one week's pay away from destitution. Bank accounts were unheard of.

To cut off a man's credit when he was out of work was unthinkable. But nobody trifled with Aunt Polly's generosity. Young Vern McAree, one of the children who came to live with Polly and John when his mother died, would tremble with fear when this tiny woman faced down a customer twice her size whom she felt was shirking his family responsibilities. Her guiding philosophy was that you shared what you had with those who "had a call on you," as opposed to indiscriminate charity. This included a former saloon keeper who had fallen on hard times when his bar was closed and he needed a pair of gloves for his bleeding hands. Polly provided them without question.

Polly believed in the special qualities of each child. She encouraged Vern McAree to keep reading, even if it were only the comics, in defiance of the local Methodist preacher who didn't approve of Vern's choice.

In 1873, Polly's sister Isabella, one of the twins and wife of the local printer, Joseph Thompson, died at the age of 28 years. The funeral took place at her home on 11 St. David Street. Polly had seen so much of suffering and death both on land and at sea, and yet once more her family's faith carried her through.

In the spring of 1880, Joseph Fleming, my grandfather's oldest brother, became the first to leave the family clan. At age 36, he went West to what is now Manitoba and set up a tent at the edge of a ravine. Such daring was par for the course for a man who had been working as a tinsmith on some of

Toronto's highest church steeples. Joseph's wife Hanna and his sons, William 6, Bert Edgar 4, and Ernest 2, travelled west by train and river craft to live in that tent for two winters.

In the summer of 1881, R. J. married his first wife, Mary Jane Breadon of Montreal. Their first child was a daughter named Reba. Not yet married two years, Mary Jane died giving birth to Everett in 1883. The widowed R.J. and his two children moved in with Polly and John, as young R.J. had when his own mother had died. "My sister Polly is a mother to my children," R.J. said to a friend. R.J. left his partnership in the coal and wood business at 2 St. David Street for the more lucrative business of real estate. Toronto was booming and he moved into an office on King Street.

Christmas Day, 1882, was one of the saddest days of Aunt Polly's life. At 3 p.m., she went to the funeral of the second of the twins born on Bridgewater Farm in Ireland, her younger sister Rebecca, who died of puerperal fever on December 23. She had raised the girl, her "special charge", and had been so excited on Rebecca's wedding day. The wedding had taken place in the living room behind the Cabbagetown store, with Rev. George Cochrane from the Wesleyan Methodist church officiating. Everyone had been excited at the store that day.

John McAree, the groom, had arrived earlier than expected and Polly had to hide him upstairs in her bedroom. She couldn't resist giving him a final lecture on taking good care of his bride, her younger sister Rebecca.

Then she rushed back downstairs to supervise the final details. Rebecca was nervous, she could tell. The dress was a little too tight at the waist. Swiftly Polly cut and pinned so that the bride could breathe. She might have known that the dressmaker was too new to follow the measurements exactly. Finally the bride was ready. Reverend Cochrane was pacing up and down. The musician was ready to begin. Polly whispered, "He's a lucky man," to the bride. They were about to begin when someone flushed the building's new toilet. There was a horrendous gushing of waters, while all the guests fell into an embarrassed silence. Then the music began. With a sigh of relief, Polly gave a gentle signal and Rebecca stepped out into married life. Within a few short years she and John had three children and imagined having an even larger family.

In January of 1883, after only a few years of marriage, Rebecca's death left John McAree to raise Vern, Caul and little Rebecca on his own. Instead of trying to raise three youngsters by himself, John and his children went to live with Aunt Polly. Uncle John fixed up the attic room for them. Three years later, little Rebecca died of diphtheria. Aunt Polly and Uncle John watched helplessly, having been told by the doctors not to give her water.

In 1886, Polly's brother R. J. was elected as alderman for St. David's Ward (later Ward 2) at the age of thirty-two. He was re-elected alderman in 1887, married Lydia Orford in 1888, and a year later was elected alderman for a third term.

In 1892, a diphtheria epidemic hit Toronto. On December 18, 1892 heavy waves caused a waterworks upheaval in Toronto Bay. This led people to drink polluted water.

In the 1890s, the whirlwind real estate speculation of the 1880s collapsed, bringing R.J. face to face with financial ruin after several successful years. Good friends tided him over, but he continued working and was able to pay back his creditors or their widows with compound interest. After three terms as an alderman, R.J. was elected mayor in 1892 with the largest majority in Toronto's history. He was known as "the people's Bob." He was elected mayor again in 1896, with William P. Hubbard, one of Canada's first politicians of African descent, elected as alderman. Throughout his career in politics, R.J.'s memory of Polly's compassion for working class families inspired his own efforts as mayor to create better conditions for the working class of the whole city.

Wanting to earn money for his family, he decided to resign part way through his term as mayor to become Assessment Commissioner at an attractive salary of $4000 a year. Later in his career he became manager of the Toronto Street Railway, another challenge for this talented man.

My mother, Victoria Fleming, was born in 1897, the year her father became Assessment Commissioner. She was named after Queen Victoria, who had just celebrated her 60th Jubilee. My mother was immediately nicknamed "Queenie" by her brothers and sisters.

In 1901 the young Vern McAree, who had been raised by Aunt Polly, became an editorial writer with the *Mail and Empire* in Toronto. He later became one of Canada's early columnists.

In 1902, John and Polly's Cabbagetown store went bankrupt. All the children whom John and Polly had taken in had grown up and left home. They sold the house and the property around it, and bought a brick house across the road from R.J. and Lydia, no doubt with their help. R.J.'s seven children were in and out of Polly's house all the time. Aunt Polly handed out homemade cookies and a strong sense of social justice.

Vern McAree became a well-respected *Globe and Mail* columnist who, according to long-time *Globe and Mail* editor Richard J. Doyle, "bashed away at bigotry, pettiness, and pomposity." Vern later wrote a small volume about Aunt Polly called *Cabbagetown Store*. When I read the book in the 1970s, I had no idea that years later I would also write a book about Aunt Polly.

I told those stories of the widow and the Cabbagetown store for the first time during a meditation talk. Just as Polly lived her life like the widow who shared what she had with Elijah, I began to see my own life as an experience of sharing whatever I had and never seeing it run out.

On April 19, 1904, fire alarm box number 31 at Bay and King Street was

Aunt Polly at her 50th wedding anniversary, November 15, 1904, wearing the Irish lace shawl given to her by her younger brother, R. J. Fleming

rung and the Great Fire of Toronto began. Flames spread from a room in E & S Currie's Neckware Plant to engulf fourteen acres in a raging holocaust that did thirteen million dollars of damage and put five thousand people out of work. Vern McAree, the young reporter for the *Mail and Empire*, wrote that Toronto's business district had been wiped out.

On July 18, 1911, my grandfather's home on St. Clair Avenue was hit by tragedy. Everett Fleming, R.J.'s closest son, suddenly dropped dead at age eighteen after suffering from heart trouble for his final three years, brought on by pneumonia. He had shared his father's love of livestock improvement and R.J. had no words to express his grief. A fellow cattle breeder said at the funeral, "He was an upright,

clever young man. He was well-known among the breeders of
Jersey cattle throughout America, some of whom predicted a
brilliant future for him in that line. He had sterling qualities,
including unfailing kindness."

Growing up, I had known nothing of my Irish heritage.
Leaving their homeland was so painful to the family that they
didn't talk about it. Even my grandfather, R.J., wrote that he
knew nothing of his Irish heritage. My cousin Bob Fleming
and his wife Patsy had made a courageous effort to find the
family farm in the midst of the thirty year Troubles in Ireland
(1968-1998). It was dangerous to travel then, but they made it
to Dromore, County Tyrone. They only had a short time to
find the farm and failed. However, Bob was able to give me the
name of our last remaining relative in Ireland, a distant cousin
named Robert Funston, who lived in Belfast. He suggested I
contact Dromore historian, Florence Corey. Just before I hung
up the phone, Bob said, "Catharine, I grew up on that farm." I
nearly dropped the phone.

In 2002, after pouring over all this family history, I set
off for Ireland to try to find the Fleming family farm that Aunt
Polly had left in 1847.

Until that time, the only information we had was
a single phrase: "on the old coach road from Dromore
to Enniskillen." So off I went to Ireland and got as far as
Enniskillen in the north. I was put on the school bus from
Enniskillen to Irvinestown, full of laughing school children
who were dropped one by one at farm lanes. After hearing
about the Troubles, this joyous trip was immensely reassuring.
The bus dropped me unceremoniously at the back door of
Mahon's Hotel in Irvinestown. The manager there suggested I
contact another noted local historian, Breege McCusker. That
Sunday, dressed in her Sunday best, Breege drove me to find

the remains of the 19th century Fleming mill, a stone set in the ground. In the 19th century, the mill had belonged to a cousin of our family, Andrew Fleming.

Catharine's hosts Thomas Corey, with his parents, Florence and Seamus,
near their farm in Ireland

From Mahon's Hotel, I phoned Florence Corey, saying I would arrive on Monday in Dromore and asking if we could meet. Florence had a busy day scheduled but she cancelled everything. On Monday morning, Florence and her husband Seamus met me at the bus stop. Seamus had been a bus driver in the English Army. He drove us to their home in nearby Shaneragh where we had lunch in their large and welcoming kitchen. Their home was a functioning farm with chickens clucking outside the window as we ate. I was welcomed to stay as their guest and the next day, Seamus drove us to find the Fleming family farm.

When I found Bridgewater farm with the Corey's help and set foot on it for the first time, there was a tremendous sensation in my body. It was as if I could hear voices that eventually gave me the words to commit the first forty pages to writing. The new owners, Evelyn and Ynr, invited me for a traditional Irish supper. Afterward, as I sat beside the peat fire, surrounded by the old stone walls, I could begin to imagine what life was like in the 1800s. I was incredibly fortunate to have experienced that old stone house, because a year later it was torn down, no longer possible to maintain.

Losing Neil in Omagh

On the next trip to Ireland, Neil came with me with an agenda of his own. One day, we set off by bus to see if we could find the birthplace of Neil's ancestors on his mother's side. We ended up in Limerick where we stayed the night. The next morning, Neil headed out to make enquiries. As I watched him walking away down the Irish street, wearing his tweed cap, I thought to myself, "He belongs."

The next day he was given directions to Coolcappa, a nearby valley. We spent the morning there, wandering around the parish graveyard in the warm rain, looking at O'Shea gravestones.

In 1821, the potato crop had failed and in 1824, Neil's O'Shea great-grandparents had walked some 100 kilometers from County Limerick to Cork Harbour, where they boarded one of six ships in the Peter Robinson Expedition of 1825 bound for Canada. Originally the British government had the wild idea of shipping two million Irish to Canada both to alleviate famine and reduce the Irish presence. Understandably, the Canadian authorities flatly refused this huge migration of people for practical reasons, as the population of Upper and

Lower Canada and Newfoundland at the time was less than 700,000. The limited expedition was subsequently organized by the Hon. Peter Robinson, Member of Parliament for York.

Carefully selected families were offered seventy acres of free land, tools and a year's supply of rations. Neil's great-grandparents, the Sheas as they came to be known without the customary O', were among those fortunate to be chosen out of thousands who applied. By a stroke of luck, I found a copy of the diary of the ship's surgeon in one of the Montreal libraries. It described the conditions at sea, the food supplies, and the daily life of the ship's passengers, including the conditions of the sick. Later, I was able to draw on that diary in recreating the journey of my own ancestors during the famine.

On the way back to stay with the Coreys, we passed through the enchanting town of Adare, renowned as one of Ireland's prettiest towns. Designated by the Irish government as a Heritage Town, many of the original houses are well-preserved examples of stone houses with thatched roofs.

We arrived in Omagh late in the evening and went to our favourite hotel. The next morning I had an errand to run at the Ulster American Folk Park, so Neil and I agreed to meet for lunch at the restaurant behind the courthouse.

I was delayed at the museum, it was pouring with rain, and there were no taxis. Seeing my predicament, a kind-hearted young woman offered to give me a lift in her truck. When I arrived at the restaurant, Neil was not there.

"He left an hour ago," the owner said. It was still lunch time, so I walked down the steep slope of Omagh's main street in the pouring rain, looking in every restaurant. No one had seen a tall Canadian in a blue jacket. By four o'clock I was in a panic. I phoned the Coreys. No call from Neil. Seamus picked me up and we searched the central area of the city. By seven o'clock we gathered at the Corey's house for a late supper.

I phoned the hospital Admissions. "Any sign of my husband?" "Dearie, you'd better phone the police." I called immediately. By midnight there was still no news.

Had Neil fallen into the river from the narrow bridge with the low railing? Had he been abducted by the IRA? A unit was known to be still operative. Dreadful scenarios filled my mind. Florence and I calmed ourselves by deciding that Neil had probably gotten caught up with the crowd going to Belfast to attend a conference with the famous Sinn Féin president, Gerry Adams, and had been unable to phone us. At our behest Seamus drove in to Omagh to meet every bus returning from the meeting. Finally we went to bed, exhausted.

The next morning at seven o'clock the phone rang. It was a young policeman. He was calling from the hotel where Neil and I had stayed. He had just found Neil in the dining room there, calmly eating breakfast and reading his newspaper.

"Sir," said the policeman, "are you lost?"

"I'm not lost," was the indignant reply. "They just haven't found me."

Seamus was not amused, to say the least, but he drove once more to Omagh to pick up the missing man.

We all sat at the Coreys kitchen table, drinking black coffee. A wave of relief turned into a current of curiosity as we waited to get the story from Neil. Having waited an hour for me for lunch, he decided I wasn't coming and went to have a look at the nearby church. There was a wedding going on that he stayed to watch.

After the wedding, he came back to the restaurant. We missed each other by minutes. He tried every Corey number in the phonebook but none of them was the right one. It turned out Seamus was ex-directory. I had the Coreys' address on me, and Neil couldn't remember it.

Finally he gave up, called a taxi and went back to our favourite hotel, had supper and went to bed.

Ten minutes after he arrived at the hotel, the young woman at the front desk went off duty, forgetting to enter Neil's name in the guest register. Her replacement therefore knew nothing of Neil when I phoned. No one but the young policeman had thought of going to the hotel to check.

In true Irish fashion, by suppertime the Corey family had turned this whole story into a joke. "You've gotten a lot of mileage out of that story," Neil later whispered wryly, as I told it standing beside him at an A.A. gathering.

The Sesostris

Fortunately, I was able to locate a book called *Irish Passenger Lists* by Brian Mitchell. As I searched for ships that left Ireland in May 1847, I scanned the names on a ship called Sesostris. Lo and behold, there were the names of my great-grandparents, William and Jane Fleming, with Polly age ten, her sister Eliza, and six other children.

To my astonishment, I was also able to locate a newspaper with a picture of the Sesostris and its time of departure from the Port of Derry. With growing excitement, I boarded a small local steamboat that retraced the passage of the Sesostris up the river from Derry and into the broad expanse of Lough Foyle, one of the safest inland harbours in Ireland.

It had occurred to me, in the early stages of writing, that Polly's dog would be called Muff. Much to my surprise, we passed a small village called Muff. As I travelled, her whole story was coming alive in detail after detail.

In Omagh, I was interviewed by the editor of the *Tyrone Constitution*, Steven McKenna. He took me all around Omagh and showed me places where fair days were held, while Pat McDonnell told me ghost stories, and Bert Duncan at *The Harp* explained the history of the Weeping Hill.

The staff at the Ulster American Folk Park and Omagh Library were a marvel. I obtained photographs of a magical small train with open carriages that travelled between Derry and Strabane.

The *Tyrone Constitution* newspaper ran a major story about my research and quoted me:

> Florence Corey, a retired history teacher, and her husband, Seamus, from Shaneragh, Dromore, drove me all over. They have taken to Polly as one of their own.
>
> I have read hundreds of editions of *Tyrone Constitution* from 1844. The paper's early pages have made the period I researched all so vivid, and many articles brought it so alive. The *Impartial Reporter* in Enniskillen and the Derry newspapers were also a great help. I even traced the notice for the sailing of the Sesostris in the *Derry Journal*. And I have got a feel for the famine, when it seems that people and clergy of all denominations came together in an extraordinary way.
>
> Mr. McGuinness, a Derry historian, spent three days with me in the city and showed me the Inishowen Peninsula and Malin Head, the last landmark the Flemings would have seen as they left Ireland for the final time.
>
> I think I have come close, too, to answering the question of what it was like, especially, for farmers to pack up and quit the county. And I'm discovering for myself what it means to be Irish, and why anyone would want to leave such a beautiful country if they didn't have to.

Like my previous two visits in 2002 and 2003, I have had to purchase an extra suitcase to transport home all the material I have accumulated. I believe I have enough material now to go ahead with the book, but I am still interested in making fresh contacts.

On my way home I stopped off in Dublin where I was interviewed extensively by Jerry Cooley for his radio show NEAR-FM. He told me that "when that Omagh bomb went off, killing all those children, we in the South said, 'We don't want to hear any more about the IRA.' As far as we were concerned, it was the end of the Troubles." I told Jerry that same terrible incident had motivated me to want our family story to be part of the healing process in Northern Ireland.

Jerry also suggested that I visit the Jeanie Johnston, a nineteenth-century sailing ship that was now lying at anchor in Dublin Harbour. I was glad indeed that I had followed his suggestion. The visit gave me a chance to better understand my own family's experience crossing the Atlantic on the Sesostris.

Jerry apparently had extensive film footage made of our conversation. I hope that at some point that footage could be made available online, as is the haunting melody on YouTube, *Polly of Bridgewater Farm*, put together by John and Scott Griffin, a father and son team whom I met in a Monahan pub.

Exploring my family roots changed my whole inner landscape, giving me a sense of belonging to a greater story that only deepens with time. All that would not have been possible without the people who turned up along the way to help: Carol Moore-Ede, who became my publisher, Seamus and Florence Corey, and so many others.

As I was writing, I had the sense at times that the story was coming through me. One time I was finishing a scene as I sat on the tiny back porch of our home on Somerville Avenue.

As I wrote the last word, I looked down in astonishment and thought, "Where did that come from?"

One of the themes that kept recurring was an image of light, even in the midst of the most tragic moments. I remembered from Sunday school, "The light shines on and the darkness cannot overcome it." It is an immense encouragement to me now, at the age of eighty-nine, to recall the variety of ways that this image kept recurring throughout my life in often unexpected ways, and is still with me.

To know with complete certainty, even in the midst of the small daily struggles and irritations that accompany each stage of life, I have not lost the vision that I was given as an eight-year-old child of a universe expanding with the Presence of love at the heart of it.

When I found that journal of the ship's surgeon who had travelled with the Peter Robinson expedition that brought Neil's mother's family to Canada in 1837, I was able to reconstruct what the journey across the Atlantic must have been like in 1847 for the 428 men, women and children on board the Sesostris, accompanied by more than a few rats.

I also found a vivid account of conditions at Grosse Île, Canada's quarantine station on June 14, 1847, the day the Sesostris arrived after thirty-one days at sea. A hospital matron had written her impressions in the *Journal de Montréal*.

> Forty ships were in quarantine with perhaps ten thousand passengers aboard, hundreds of whom were sick. They could not be taken ashore, however, because of the lack of sheds. I set to work pitching tents for sick people whose condition seemed most promising. Even if I had wanted to provide shelter for those whose recovering looked doubtful, I would not have had room for one-tenth of them.

There must have been so much hopeful and sad energy on the shores at Grosse Île. Neil and I went there twice, where we met Marianna O'Gallagher who worked to preserve Grosse Île as an Irish monument. She showed us the sheds and the location of the tents where Polly's sister Eliza had become ill with typhus, leading to her death. We also saw the location of some of the horrifying mass graves where so many Irish were buried.

Grosse Île is an island of terror and beauty, and Marianna O'Gallagher's books have helped preserve the history. When I look at what I have written about that part of our family's story, it is as though history is coming through me, the past being healed in the present, with the help of so many people on both sides of the Atlantic.

It was an extraordinary moment for me to visit Aunt Polly's grave for the first time in St. James Cemetery in Toronto, accompanied by my cousin John Fleming and dream daughter Stéphanie. There also was the grave of Polly's mother, my great-grandmother, Jane Caldwell Noble. I returned to Montreal and plunged into the complicated task of writing a book on Ireland while living in Canada. Goethe's statement that "when you take on an impossible task, the universe conspires to help you" was no doubt drawn from his own experience. I've come back to that sentence many times.

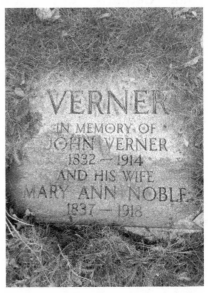

Gravestone of Polly Verner and her husband in St. James Cemetery in Toronto

Adventures with Neil

Neil was supportive of my efforts throughout this time, no longer fussing about me being away for periods of time or occasionally being late. As always, he could make me laugh.

One winter night, I set the table for supper and placed small candles at various angles to provide us with some cheerful light. I had cooked a shepherd's pie, which I placed in front of him so that he could serve us both.

Neil was wearing his fuzzy, warm red dressing gown over a long sleeved shirt and pants, his usual in the winter evenings. As he reached across the table to hand me my plate, one of the sleeves of his dressing gown caught fire. He must have seen the look in my eyes and got up quietly from his chair. "Catharine, don't panic," he said and walked toward the kitchen. I followed him and thought: Water! The sink! But the sink was too far away. Instead I grabbed a big green canister of flour from the counter, yanked off the lid and threw the flour over Neil.

Luckily, the flour didn't explode and the flames went out. Neil, covered with flour, went calmly back to the dining room, sat down at his place and, resting his left arm on the table, lifted up the first mouthful with his right, while I collapsed into my chair opposite him, laughing hysterically. I'm not aware whether his arm was burned because, if it were, he never said anything. His reaction and his advice have stood me in good stead on many occasions since. "Catharine, don't panic."

One day, to my surprise, Neil announced that he and his A.A. buddy Jim were going to build a shed in our garden. Together they picked up the materials and, with a fair amount of heaving, assembled them in the back yard. The completed shed was affixed to the back wall of our house, between the window and the porch entrance. Finally we had a proper place for our garden tools, instead of having to lug them up from the basement. Neil showed me the final product with great satisfaction. They also brought flower plants from the market. That summer our garden radiated with colour and our little squirrel once again turned somersaults of joy.

Because of his difficulty sleeping, Neil had moved out of our room at the front of the house, with its big double bed, into a small room next to the bathroom.

One night at about four a.m., I was woken by a terrific crash. I shoved my feet into my slippers and hurried into the hall to see what had happened. I discovered that after getting off the toilet Neil had fallen right through the shower curtain and was flat on his back in the empty bathtub right next to the toilet.

"I'm not hurt," he said, "so help me up." For an hour we tried, but to no avail. Finally I phoned Westmount Security up the hill and within a few minutes, two strong men arrived. With little trouble, they hauled Neil safely onto his feet, out of the bathtub and into his bed. I kissed him goodnight and went thankfully back to bed.

At about seven in the morning, I heard a dull thud from the bedroom next door. Neil had slid out of his bed and onto the floor.

"I think I must have mixed up one of my medications," he said rather sleepily. Once again I called Westmount Security and they helped me get Neil downstairs and onto the living room couch. "You'd better call 911," one of the men said to me. "Will you do it for me?" I whispered. "He'll have a fit if I do. I'll fix him some breakfast." While I was in the kitchen making coffee, I heard a siren. A fire engine came roaring onto our cosy street with the siren blasting at full throttle, jolting awake most of our neighbours. Next came an ambulance, again with siren blasting needlessly. Two men came in the front door, carrying a stretcher. I pointed to the living room and went back to the kitchen.

In a few moments, one of the men came out to the kitchen. "Mrs. McKenty, my wife listens to your husband all the time and I do when I can. We have great admiration for him, but I am unable to persuade him to go to the hospital and by law we can't force him. I'm sorry." I heaved a sigh, showed them to the door, and fried us both some eggs and bacon.

Neil camped out on the sofa for the next two days, his legs unable to get up the stairs. Clearly he'd had a small stroke of some kind. I made meals, organized a porta-toilet since there was no bathroom on the first floor, and ordered Neil's favourite lamb chops from the Toucheh Restaurant at the corner. Our kind friend Ahdi Montebassen brought them right to the door. They had been cooked to perfection by his brother Mehdi who had been a chef in an Italian restaurant for 15 years, before the family of Mehdi, Ahdi and Azita took over this restaurant.

On the third morning, after another night on the couch, Neil gave a sigh and said, "Catharine, I suppose I had better go to the hospital." I took a deep breath, brought Neil his clothes and phoned 911.

Once again an ambulance with siren at full blast arrived at our front door. Neil walked calmly out the front door and over to the ambulance. The startled attendant said, "Mr. McKenty, you're the healthiest looking patient I have ever picked up." Neil muttered to me over his shoulder as he kept walking, "Catharine, we should have done this several days ago." I could have killed him.

Catharine in Ireland signing books at the launch of
Polly of Bridgewater Farm, 2009

REVIEW OF POLLY OF BRIDGEWATER FARM

In 2009, the biography of my Irish Aunt Polly was
published. In 2010 Alice Abracen published a review of *Polly
of Bridgewater Farm* in *The Senior Times*, which was reprinted

two years later in *Irish Connections Canada*. Excerpts from Abracen's review read:

> It is with great pleasure that I introduce a book that is not only a lively and enjoyable read, but also even if our own family recollections have long since vanished, allows us to retake our ancestors' journey through the eyes of a young girl who endured a similar voyage.
>
> *Polly of Bridgewater Farm: An Unknown Irish Story* allows complete strangers to connect with the voices of their own past.
>
> The novel opens with two young people witnessing the burning of Montreal's Parliament by disgruntled Tories (a part of our city's history that many seem to have forgotten), destroying its chances of becoming a capital city. These are Polly Noble and her future husband, John Verner, and the year is 1849.
>
> The book is a swift and pleasant read, the prose at once lyrical and accessible, the pages rife with illustrations, photographs and maps. It is a journey immensely worth undertaking.

To my delight, the book is now available at the Centre for Peace and Reconciliation in Northern Ireland, just south of Derry.

In 2010, Neil and I attended the 50th wedding anniversary party of our friends Bob and Denise McCormick, north of Montreal. All went well as we drove north, then we came to a crossroad. "Go right," I said confidently. Naturally Neil turned left. Eventually I got us back on track and we ended up dancing and having a lot of fun.

In September 2011, we sold our Somerville Avenue house and moved into a marvellous seniors' residence, the Manoir Westmount, right next to Victoria Hall and the Westmount Library. For nearly forty years we had lived in the original farmhouse on Somerville Avenue, just five blocks away. Moving into the Manoir Westmount turned out to be a gift for both Neil and myself.

CATHARINE, BE HAPPY

We went back up to the Laurentian Lodge Club, spent sunny days skiing out in the woods, with white clouds sailing overhead and without the dark clouds in our minds. Then we returned home to supper in our cozy residence. A simple mantra surfaced in my mind with no conscious effort on my part. Just five words that kept repeating themselves: "I'm so happy with Neil." We even managed to take one more Senior Tour on a cruise ship. It was a happy time.

During the days after our return, I noticed a change, a return of the dark energy. Concerned, I persuaded Neil to see Dr. Roper. Dr. Roper whispered to me that Neil had stopped taking one of his meds because he felt so well. Next came a consultation with Dr. Cervantes. He increased the medication enough to make sure there was no return of the suicidal impulse.

In May of 2012, Neil was due to go with Jim to the annual A.A. weekend get-together of a group of men at the Mad River Barn down in Vermont. It was an outing he always enjoyed. I didn't want to leave Neil on his own for any length of time but this looked like a window of time around which I could build a short trip to Ireland. I booked a plane ticket.

The day before I was to leave, Neil told me he had decided not to go to the weekend. "I'm not feeling quite up to scratch," he said with no further explanation. When he saw my look of concern, he added firmly, "But don't cancel your trip." So off I went to a warm welcome at Thomas Corey's home. As usual I stayed in what Thomas had dubbed "Catharine's room."

When Thomas built the house, I was the first one to stay there overnight. In the meadow a donkey nodded a welcome and the little dog, Sammy, wagged his tail in a friendly hello when he came over for a visit.

Three days after my arrival, I was awakened in the middle of the night by the sound of voices and a gentle hand on my shoulder. It was Florence Corey, with Seamus standing beside her. "It's Clare Hallward on the phone for you, Catharine."

I listened to the call with growing apprehension. On Saturday morning, Clare had gone to the Manoir Westmount to take Neil a book she had promised him. There was no answer when she knocked on the door of his room. She learned from the nurse on duty that he had been taken to the hospital. She was calling me from there now. Neil was unconscious and they were doing their best to resuscitate him.

Hurriedly I dressed and packed with Florence's help. We called a taxi which took me straight to the airport. I booked the next flight out and sat in a daze, dozing off and on. The flight got me to Boston, where I had no choice but to wait at the airport hotel for my connection four hours later.

I went straight to the hospital where I found Clare and the surgeon. "I don't think there's much more we can do for him," he said to me. Neil had written his "do not resuscitate" order very clearly, and I had to respect that. All the tubes were removed. Fortunately, one procedure had been done when he arrived that allowed Neil to continue breathing as long as his heart allowed. He was moved out of intensive care and into a single room down a quiet hall.

Clare insisted that I stay at her apartment just down the road from the hospital. That first night I was able to walk up to the hospital and sit by Neil's bed for three hours. Over the next four days, the young people who had worked with him in radio and television visited. I was touched by the deep concern shown by each of them.

There was no room for Neil in the palliative care unit, but Anne Hallward came up from her therapy practice in Maine and used all her medical skills to make sure he was comfortable. Stéphanie came and washed his sad feet, damaged from the cheap shoes he wore.

Neil never regained consciousness. On the sixth night, I sat beside him singing a little song over and over, "You're on your way, darling man, you're on your way." An old friend from the Pine Avenue meditation centre, Mary Francine Joron, joined Anne that night, and around midnight they insisted I go home and get some sleep. Before I left, I said to Neil, "Send me a message if you can." I had heard of that happening. About three a.m. Neil stopped breathing and slipped quietly into the next phase of his life. He was eighty-seven. It turned out his kidneys had failed. I heard the news in the morning.

The next hours were full of decisions to be made. They remain something of a blur. Clare was kindness itself and my cousin John Fleming a stalwart counsellor. Neil's ashes were to be buried with my parents in Mount Pleasant Cemetery in Toronto, where there was room for mine, too. John advised cremation straight from the hospital.

I arranged for the urn with the ashes to be placed in a wooden casket for the Irish wake and the funeral the next day. That evening, Irish music was provided by Patrick Hutchison, founder of the Swift Years Irish band. Friends came and went, the music reminding me of all our wonderful times in Ireland. At one point, the music picked up and I looked over to see a third person playing, a friend who had gone home to fetch his instrument. He spent the rest of the evening with us.

At the funeral the next day, the music was provided by my cousin Everett Fleming, with his special ability to play piano by ear, allowing him to reset the hymn in a key we could all manage. Our long-time friend from the Priory days, Paul Geraghty, conducted the service. The casket I rented provided a background for the special ceremony of blessing, the swinging of the incense. I remember sitting there feeling sheer exhaustion and stress to the point that I nearly passed out. Suddenly I heard Neil's voice! Clare's daughter Anne Hallward had recorded Neil for her radio show *Safe Space* in the United States and I heard him saying, "There is nothing to fear about death." His voice gave me the energy I needed to get through the rest of the day.

At the reception afterward, our tiny friend whom we had met on a trip to Israel, Dolores Kumps, came up to me and said, "Catharine, I had the most amazing dream last night. There was Neil large as life. He said to me, 'Dolores, be happy.'" As soon as I heard that, I thought, "He's done it. He's sent me a message."

I've done my best ever since to follow that instruction, but that night I was all alone in Neil's room back at the residence. I was just about to break down completely when three words came into my mind unbidden, "Grateful beyond measure."

It was only many years later that I discovered the source of that phrase. I was visiting my cousin Ross in Toronto. He said, "Catharine, I've been working on Dad's papers. Marguerite van Die, the historian, came to have a look at them. There is one letter she thought I should give you and here it is."

When I read it, I was speechless. There was the phrase. It was my mother writing to her brother, Goldie, who had driven through the night from Lake Simcoe to be with her when I was born. It was written just after Dad's death in that car accident.

Dear Goldie,

...I am determined not to go under. I feel a spiritual
strength being given. I am grateful beyond measure.

That phrase must have been present in my life,
consciously or not, from my earliest days. Tears of gratitude
well up as I write, gratitude for the strength and courage of
my mother whose faith sustained both of us. I had written
her a letter a few years after my marriage to Neil, describing
my gratitude for her faith and courage. After her death I
found that letter in her drawer. She had written on it "MORE
PRECIOUS THAN GOLD."

After Neil's death, the phrase "I'm so happy with Neil,"
transformed itself into, "I'm so happy *about* Neil." Indeed I
was. No more pain or risk of mood swings. Free at last. I could
talk to him, certain that in some mysterious way he would be
looking out for me.

I ask myself how on earth I was able to navigate
alongside my husband all those years, with the unexpected
twists and turns. I can't help thinking how much I owe my
Irish and Scottish ancestors. On Mum's side, the family
members who made that perilous journey across Atlantic in
1847 in the middle of the Great Famine of 1845-49. On Dad's
side, the courage of those three brothers who founded a school
in India. Dad's perilous journey on foot in South America.
Mum's courage to carry on after his death. The example of the
courageous people I met in postwar Europe.

From all these people and imbedded in my genes came
the certainty that we must not give up in difficult times.
Beyond that was a profound sense that had expressed itself in
a dream one night after Neil's depression had lifted.

The Universe Cares About Us

Shortly after the depression had lifted, I had fallen fast asleep in my cozy room at the Manoir. Gradually I felt myself running. Then I crossed a road in the pitch-black darkness, with vehicles coming straight at me from both directions. I ran straight across, arriving miraculously on the other side without harm.

Next, I ran along a dark, silent road with only the sound of the wind accompanying me and the footsteps of a courageous friend. I came out onto an avenue of beech trees, their branches bending down toward me, the leaves full of light and warmth. When I came to the end of that avenue, I ran up to a straggly group of people standing at the bus stop. Breathlessly, I blurted out a single sentence, "I have just one thing to say: the universe cares about us!" That's been a recurring theme in my life, and also in my husband's, although there were times when it may not have seemed so.

Barbara Moser, Publisher of *The Senior Times*, wrote the following tribute to Neil:

> Neil McKenty began a relationship with *The Senior Times* in May 1998. He developed an avid following because of his integrity, his meticulous research and his strong and grounded opinions.
>
> He championed those politicians who displayed his own passions for the rights of the marginalized in North American societies.
>
> He had no patience for hypocrites and double dealers. That's why readers awaited for his monthly "Pit Stop" as did his editors, myself included.
>
> I was proud to have Neil as one of ours. He raised the bar and set the standard for engaging and thought-provoking journalism.

Over the years, Neil's writing helped shaped *The Senior Times*, always reflecting our values and concerns as a newspaper.

We will miss him dearly and send our heartfelt condolences to his loving wife of 40 years, Catharine.

Irwin Block of *The Senior Times* followed Barbara's tribute to Neil with his own:

Intellectual rigour was always the basis of his structured viewpoints on a range of subjects.

McKenty had his demons. He battled depression and wrote about it in his candid autobiography, *The Inside Story,* in which he recalls his struggle to reconcile his profound religious beliefs and his need to fully express himself as a human being. He did that with great eloquence and his voice, which echoes among his many followers, will be missed by all.

Years later, I picked up the twentieth anniversary issue of *The Senior Times* from 2006, with Pops from Dans La Rue and other well-known Montrealers on the cover. As I flipped through the paper, a headline caught my eye. "McKenty, he's edgy, he's provocative and he's ours." Way to go, Barbara.

An obituary by Alan Hustak, Neil's friend for fifty years, was printed in the *Montreal Gazette*. He opened his text with the sentence, "Neil McKenty liked to argue for the hell of it...he moderated, infuriated, provoked and entertained his listeners and a host of readers."

After Neil's death, I began working on a book about Neil. With the help of Richard Rice, a substantial text, complete with pictures, began to emerge. The text kept growing and growing. I had newspaper articles galore about my husband. Then there were all the reviews of the books he had written. Five hundred pages later, my brain was about to fry.

Miraculously, Alan Hustak hove into sight at that moment. He had written that brief and effective obituary in the *Montreal Gazette* for Neil. At one point, he had even thought of writing a biography of his long-time friend. Now he said, "Let's see what you've got."

Next thing I knew, Alan had taken the enormous pile of material and zipped through it with the speed and expertise of his years as an editor and a writer. The result was *Neil McKenty Live*, the kind of book anyone could pick up, even if they had never heard Neil on the radio or read anything he had written. I felt tremendous gratitude to Alan for this major achievement.

The book was well-reviewed and travelled with me to the mental health conference in Toronto, where the opening event for the next five years would be the Neil McKenty Memorial Lecture, thanks to copies of Neil's memoir I had sent them earlier.

My Last Day in Ireland, 2015

In 2015, on my last day in Ireland, Seamus Corey drove Florence and me up to Pigeon Top, with its view over the hills to the rooftops of Omagh. I got out of the car and stood there, breathing in the pure air. The strangest feeling came over me. I was not leaving Ireland for the last time. There was no need to grieve. I had always been there. I always would be. I got back in the car and we headed for the airport.

The Spider

Since I moved with my husband to this seniors' residence, I've often been asked if I felt cooped up, checked upon, even imprisoned. I've always answered, "No, quite the contrary. We come and go freely." Then I remembered one evening. I was doing some writing. It was 10:30 at night. When I went to my door to turn off the light, I noticed a small creature ambling along the carpet. It was a tiny spider. I scooped him up in a glass jar, put the lid on it, and took the elevator downstairs.

My plan was to put him safely out on the grass outside the Manoir. As I walked towards the front door, a firm voice behind me said, "Mrs. McKenty, where do you think you are going at this hour of the night?" No doubt the attendant thought I was losing my marbles! When I explained, we had a good laugh. Then I continued on my way. Just at that moment, two old friends happened to walk by on their way home. I asked them to complete my mission. The little spider was safely stowed among the lovely trees on the far side of the driveway. I returned happily to bed, glad that my sanity had been established.

Riding My Own Elephant

On the morning of my eighty-eighth birthday, Stéphanie arrived with the cutest toy dog I have ever seen, accompanied by a note from each of my dream daughters. This little dog was promptly adopted as a sister by my other stuffed toy dog, Muttsi. I named her Dreamy. She often brightens up our dining room table when there are no flowers, to the amusement of other residents.

In a recent conversation, one of my dream daughters, Laurie, asked about the title of this book. *Riding the Elephant* reminded her of the time she herself had ridden an elephant when a circus came to town. "It gives you a feeling of power," she said. "It reminds me of the time when I was working at L'Arche. We used to place the handicapped children up on a large, slow-moving, well-trained horse. It gave those children a sense of empowerment they had never experienced.

Catharine at the Manoir Westmount's
2018 Halloween party

"That's what your grandmother passed on to you. And your Aunt Ev who triumphed over her fears to become a surgeon in India. It was unusual for women in the Thirties to do what the women in your family did. The strength they passed on to you played a key role in your life with Neil. During those forty years with him, you rode your own elephant, dealing with your own fears."

NEIL MAKES ME LAUGH

There is no question that the years with Neil were both a rich and a dangerous journey for me, both physically and emotionally. Yet what astonishes me is that I was *given* the strength. I was *given* the love. I think of it as the love at the heart of the universe, pouring itself through each of us to give to one another.

Listening to a tape of John Main answering questions, he spoke of entering into the prayer of Jesus to the Father.

It strikes me now that all pure, unconditional love, including the love against all odds that I had for Neil, enters into that universal prayer of Jesus to the Father. We learn from that experience to stop being hard on ourselves and others. To let go of grudges, to remember the words of Jesus on the cross, "Father, forgive them, for they know not what they do."

I was rereading Neil's "Author's Note" at the beginning of his memoir, *The Inside Story*. He wrote, "Many have helped me on this journey, but I will only mention here my wife, Catharine, to whom this memoir is dedicated and without whose love and support I should not have survived."

As I reread those last ten words, the tears welled up, as they did the first time, when I was completely stunned.

Then I began to laugh. I thought about all the adventures, the ups and downs, and I realized he'd done it again. He'd made me laugh when I least expected it, as he had when he sat down calmly to eat supper, his red dressing gown plastered with flour.

As I arrive at the closing lines of twenty years of writing and recall, my question is: have I done justice to the courage of this man? Have I made it clear how proud I was to have been the wife of this extraordinary, brave and talented human being? The difficulties seem less and less important and I take comfort from the friend in Al-Anon who said, we do the best we can.

THE STORY-GATHERER

The following poem was written for me by my friend Nick Schnitzer on my eighty-eighth birthday. I was profoundly moved when I discovered that the poem had been included in the collection of his poetry for his funeral on January 25, 2019.

The Story-Gatherer

This day remembers the story of your birth

A day with a special number

This day marking 80 plus eight years of your story

This day treasures your story

This day celebrates you, the storyteller

You follow the path of your ancestors

From the land of storytellers

Your ancestors passed on the stories of the ancient Celts

You are a "story-gatherer"

Harvesting the stories of all who cross your path

Sharing your treasure

With all who travel your path

This day is grateful for your gift

Of gathering and telling stories

Happy Birthday, Catharine

Your love of stories is contagious.

ACKNOWLEDGMENTS

My heartfelt thanks to Alan Hustak, who encouraged me on the arduous journey of doing justice to my own story alongside Neil; Clare Hallward, my friend for sixty-five years, who typed and cheered at tough moments; Stéphanie Pagano, whose enthusiasm for and practical help with this project allowed me to relax; Jeri Pitzel, who saved my sanity during continuing days of editorial effort. Jeri seized the essence of the story, added clarity and dovetailed details; the management and staff of the Manoir Westmount, who provided a supportive environment; the residents who listened to my stories, providing a steady testing ground as they took their final shape; Joan Samuels, who praised the stories, edited intelligently and brought me three of the latest comprehensive books on bipolar disorder; John Fleming, a tireless cheerleader from day one, who edited intelligently and kept my finances in order so I could concentrate on writing; Tim Brierley, whose expert editing got me off to a good start; last and far from least, Wally and Betty Turnbull who already published brand new editions of all our books. They brought their expertise to bear to bring this project to fruition. Wally filled in family details I had not known.

CATHARINE McKENTY

Catharine McKenty grew up on her grandparents' farm, "Donlands," then eight miles outside the Toronto city limits on Don Mills Road. She went in every day to Bishop Strachan School, where she won scholarships in French and German. After taking a degree in English at Victoria College, University of Toronto, she spent four winters as a volunteer in the

Courtesy Frank Greene

mining area of post-war Germany with an international group of young people involved in reconstruction.

Catharine served as Research Editor for *Pace*, a magazine for young people, based in Los Angeles and New York, and linked with the international musical group *Up With People.*

Next came a stint as a speechwriter for the Ontario Minister of Education in Toronto. At that time she met her future husband, author-broadcaster Neil McKenty on the dance floor.

Catharine worked at the *Reader's Digest;* she published *Polly of Bridgewater Farm: An Unknown Irish Story*; worked alongside Neil on the biography of John Main; and with Neil co-authored a best-seller on the early days of Laurentian skiing: ***Skiing Legends and the Laurentian Lodge Club.***

OTHER MCKENTY BOOKS

THE INSIDE STORY
MEMOIR BY NEIL MCKENTY

A book for anyone on the journey to wholeness. A story of toxic religion, sex and celibacy, drinking and depression, and how they led towards self-discovery and spiritual awakening. "A compelling testimony to our capacity for spiritual transformation in the face of overwhelming odds. McKenty's story

is both inspirational and gut-wrenchingly honest. Highly recommended."
—Tom Harpur,
Syndicated Columnist and Bestselling Author

THE OTHER KEY
A DETECTIVE NOVEL BY NEIL MCKENTY

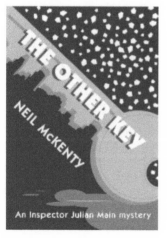

It was January 4, 2003, when Inspector Julian Main was jolted from a deep sleep by his telephone ringing, like a warning. Groggily, he looked at his watch. 2:15. His mouth felt dry and rancid like sour wine. 'Commander Durocher, here, Inspector. I've just been informed that Louise Branson, the wealthy socialite, has been murdered in her home at 76 Forden Road in Westmount. I want you to take charge of the case and I think you should get over there right away.' For the next two months, Inspector Main, Homicide Division, Montreal Police, tracked the killer like a leopard stalking a gazelle. The hunt took him to London, where he had been attached to Scotland Yard, and to Dublin, where his sister had been sexually assaulted. In the end it brought him back to Montreal where he and his sidekick, the gum chewing Detective Roy Marchand, uncover the other key.

IN THE STILLNESS DANCING:
THE JOURNEY OF JOHN MAIN BY NEIL MCKENTY

Journalist, soldier, barrister and Benedictine monk, John Main's spiritual odyssey was a deep-seated quest for an authentic life of prayer. The door finally opened when he met an Indian swami who taught him to meditate using a mantra, only to close again when he entered the Benedictine noviciate and adopted a more traditional form of prayer.

Long after ordination in 1963, John Main discovered that the form of prayer advocated by the swami already existed within the mainstream of Western Christianity but had fallen into disuse. From then on, he was to devote his life to restoring this form of Christian meditation to its rightful place within the Church. His work began with the foundation of a meditation centre at Ealing Abbey in London and led, some years later, to the foundation of the Benedictine Priory of Montreal and the establishment of a worldwide spiritual family linked through the daily practice of meditation.

Neil McKenty paints an attractive portrait of this compelling Irish monk whose teaching and writing on meditation were to transform the lives of thousands of men and women.

POLLY OF BRIDGEWATER FARM
BY CATHARINE FLEMING MCKENTY

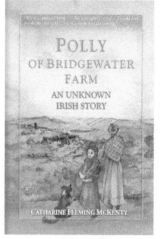

A true story of hope amidst the adversity of the Irish famine of the 1840s and emigration to Canada.

How in the world did Polly Noble, a bubbly little girl with freckles, born just outside Dromore in January 1837, live to become the subject of a biography published more than a century later in Toronto?

It was on her father's farm, on the old Coach Road between Dromore and Enniskillen, that Polly spent two years with her parents, George and Jane Noble. Then disaster struck. On January 6, 1839, the Big Wind rose out of the sea and swept across Ireland, wailing like a thousand banshees. It flattened whole villages, burned down farm houses, and finally killed her father. It changed Polly's life forever.

Two years later, Polly's mother, Jane, married William Fleming, the handsome widower across the road at Bridgewater Farm. Soon Polly began to walk back and forth the mile or so to the one-room school run in Dromore by the Kildare Society. But she also found time to plant potatoes, milk the cows, look after the goats, pull flax, chase the hens and run bare-foot in the meadows.

Then disaster struck again. The potato crop failed and the famine and typhus threatened Bridgewater Farm. Like thousands of others the Flemings decided they must escape. They packed what they could, travelling by horse and cart to Londonderry/Derry, and drinking in their last views of the green fields and hills of Ireland. On May 14, 1847, along with 418 other passengers, they boarded the three-masted sailing ship 'Sesostris'.

Only 10 years old, Polly was on her way to a new life in Canada. After an appalling voyage, during which some of the passengers died, including Polly's darling little brother and sister, they docked at Grosse-Île, the quarantine station on the St. Lawrence River, about an hour from Quebec. After three years in Montreal, where she met her future husband, Polly was now ready for her next adventure in a vast unknown land called Canada. Her destiny would be linked with a dozen children who had lost their mothers, one of them a future mayor of Toronto.

McKenty Live!
The Lines Are Still Blazing

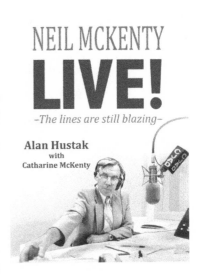

NEIL MCKENTY
LIVE!
–The lines are still blazing–

Alan Hustak
with
Catharine McKenty

Neil McKenty liked to argue just for the hell of it. During the 1970s and 80s he was one of Montreal's highest rated radio talk show hosts with 76,000 listeners. "If I bore my listeners, I'm dead." This collection of colourful stories and articles, by and about Neil, highlight his radio talk-show and his writing ability. It includes previously unpublished pieces and Aislin cartoons.

SKIING LEGENDS AND THE LAURENTIAN LODGE CLUB

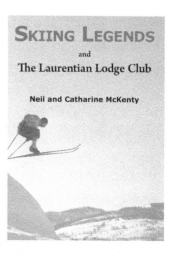

This book invites you to curl up beside the fire and journey to a time when Montrealers skied down Peel Street and the Laurentians were "the wild west" of Quebec.

There we meet skiing legends like "Jackrabbit" Johannsen, Harry Pangman and Barbara Kemp. With them we discover the perils of "Foster's Folly", the world's first ski tow. We climb Mont-Tremblant in the Thirties and we ride the ski trains with their smell of wax, orange peels and cigar smoke. And we also meet those earlier legends, the larger-than-life Curé Labelle, and the tragic Viscount d'Ivry who lived in a magnificent chateau on the shores of Lac-Manitou. This is also the story of how the Laurentians helped Montrealers weather two World Wars and the Depression—it's a great story! *Winner of the 2002 Skade Award for best skiing history (Vail, Colorado).*

For additional information visit:

www.flemingmckentyexchange.com

www.neilmckenty.com

www.torchflamebooks.com/catharine-mckenty

CPSIA information can be obtained
at www.ICGtesting.com
Printed in the USA
LVHW050707290819
629173LV00004BA/6/P

9 781611 533460